HOW TO HAVE A FLOOD
AND NOT DROWN

HOW
TO HAVE
A FLOOD
AND
NOT DROWN

Essays on Stress-Free Living

Barbara King

DeVorss & Company, *Publishers*
BOX 550, MARINA DEL REY, CA 90294–0550

All Scripture references are taken from the King James Version of the Bible, unless otherwise noted.

ISBN: 0-87516-625-3

Printed in the United States of America

DEDICATION

These writings are lovingly dedicated to my son, Michael Lewis King, who continues to teach and remind me to let go and let God.

Contents

Foreword

No matter the pressing human need, God can meet it on time and always in the most appropriate way. Why is this so? Because we are unique expressions of God, and God, as the Larger Field of Consciousness, is always working to see to our highest good.

We may have doubts. We may have challenges. No matter—as soon as we open the mind and heart to the Larger Reality, It will respond. God looks after us even when we fail to turn our attention to Him. How much more can God work His miracles in our lives when we are responsive to His will!

The principles of mind and consciousness are exact. All we have to do is learn to relate to them correctly. All we have to do is allow the mind to be renewed so that the activity of the Holy Spirit can work the transforming wonders.

I have known Barbara King for several years and have worked with her in organizational meetings as well as on the church platform. I can testify that she

is an embodiment of that which she teaches so well.
I am certain that she speaks and writes with spiritual
authority because she walks with the Father.

> Roy Eugene Davis
> Director
> Center for Spiritual Awareness

Preface

We hear a lot these days about stress and "coping skills." As far as I'm concerned, however, one of the best jobs of coping with stress was the one Daniel did in the lions' den!

I believe in the miracle of Daniel in the lions' den because I've seen what man calls "impossible" become the *possible* with God. But to fully understand this story, we have to go beyond the literal events and look at the symbolism. For instance, imagine yourself as Daniel; your den is your mind. When within your mind you have thoughts of fear, of worry, of disgust, of hate, of anger, these emotions become the lions of your den.

So what do you do about it? Daniel was known as a man who prayed three times a day. When he was thrown into the lions' den, all he had to do was to go back to the truths of God. Now perhaps we don't have outer lions, but oh, do we have *inner* ones! They are eating at us, gnawing at us, tearing us apart. At such times, the thing to do is exactly

what Daniel did: go to our Father and pray for Him
to shut the mouths of the lions. When you go to God
about a situation, all that fear and worry *has* to get
out of your mind, because remember, we know scien-
tifically, we know psychologically, that two conflict-
ing ideas cannot occupy the mind at the same time.

What this means is that the story of Daniel in the
lions' den, when viewed symbolically, is just as valid
today as when it was recorded in the Old Testament.
Likewise, the story of Noah and the Great Flood has
a modern-day application, as you will see in Chapter
One. The people of Daniel's and Noah's times were
no different from you and me, and neither were their
problems. They too wrestled with family relationships, taxes, romantic involvements, self-esteem,
money, success in business, war, diseases, poverty,
oppression, crime. You name it, they knew it!

Still, through all that mankind has or has not
done, there has always been a loving, forgiving
Father-Mother God. (We say "Father-Mother God"
because since everything was created from this one
source, then clearly both male and female are con-
tained within It.) And that Father-Mother God has
always been just one prayer away. Prayer is all that
it takes to shut the mouths of lions; prayer is all that

it takes to bring into your heart and mind a cleansing flood that will clear your inner landscape and let you plant new, healthy seeds.

Whatever you are facing, don't let God be the last place you turn. As you will find in the pages of this book, you can save yourself a great deal of time and agony if you turn to God for whatever coping you have to do and seek Him first in all things.

CHAPTER ONE

Do I Need a Flood?

In truth we believe that the Scriptures have a message for us today. Although we are not living in the times of Noah, we can recognize the symbolic meaning of his experiences and those of the other men and women of the Bible. Their experiences are ours at a different level, a level of consciousness. From their overcoming of hardships, for instance, we can know that we too can overcome any condition in our lives.

When you saw the title of this chapter, you probably reacted to it at face value. The *flood* brings to mind a large mass of water; we think of it rushing and filling up an area and being destructive. But we don't *always* use the word *flood* to refer to the physical, forceful movement of water. It can also suggest an *idea;* and I praise God for His ideas, for this is the way He speaks to us. I want you, then, to think

1

of this symbolic meaning of the word *flood* and to let it suggest to you an internal flood that we are often in need of. But let's examine the Scriptures first to get a clear understanding of the flood that Noah himself experienced.

In the fifth verse of the sixth chapter of Genesis, we read:

> And God saw that the wickedness of man was great in the earth, and that every imagination of the thoughts of his heart was only evil continually.

What has happened here is that God has seen that the mind of man was not a mind with God abiding in it; and in seeing the negativity of His created people, He decided to flood the earth, to completely wash out this negativity. Noah, however, was a man who walked with God. Therefore, he and his family were spared.

Speaking through the mind of Noah, God gave him instructions as to what he should do to prepare for the flood. He instructed Noah first to build an ark of a certain length, breadth, and kind of wood. He also gave Noah very particular instructions about how the ark was to be constructed. The next thing

God instructed Noah to do was to take his wife, his sons and their wives, and two of every living creature into the ark.

Now as Noah built his ark, the people around him were probably making fun of him. He's got to be crazy, they said, building an ark, talking about a flood. But Noah continued following that inner guidance, that direction as to what he was to do.

When the ark was completed, Noah moved his family and a male and female of every living species into the craft. And then, in Genesis 7:10-11: *"And it came to pass after seven days, that the waters of the flood were upon the earth. . . . [and] all the fountains of the great deep [were] broken up, and the windows of heaven were opened."*

In other words, not only was there a deluge of rain from the skies, but the oceans, lakes, rivers, and streams of the land were also let loose. The flooding continued for forty days and forty nights, and then, *"God made a wind to pass over the earth, and the waters assuaged; the fountains also of the deep and the windows of heaven were stopped, and the rain from heaven was restrained"* (Genesis 8:1-2). In the meantime, however, all the living creatures of the earth were destroyed except Noah and his family and the pairs of species which he had taken into the ark.

It took ten months for the waters to recede from the earth; and then, forty days later, after the ark had come to rest on the mountaintop, Noah was again intuitively led, this time to open the window of the ark and to send forth a raven. The raven flew back and forth across the face of the earth until the water began seeping into the land. Noah then released a dove, but the dove returned because there was not yet a dry spot upon the ground.

Seven days later, Noah sent the dove out again; this time she came back bearing an olive branch. By this sign, Noah knew that the land was dry. Still, he waited another seven days and then sent the dove forth again. This time the dove did not return, and so he knew that it was all right for him and his family and the animals to come out of the ark.

Noah's first act upon leaving the ark was to build a tabernacle and to offer thanks to the Lord God. And God told him, *I'm making a covenant with you, Noah, that a flood will never again destroy the earth.* The sign of the covenant was a rainbow, its different colors being a spiritual representation of God's truth, a symbol of His saying that His truth will always abide on earth and that so long as man lives by it, he will never again have to go through an experience like Noah's.

OUR KINSHIP WITH NOAH

Now let's look at the symbolic meaning of the word *flood* and see how it applies to you and me. Many of us go through our daily experience harboring in our minds any number of negative thoughts. When this happens, it's because we have forgotten that we are not just human, but that we are also Divine. There is that spirit of us, that higher self, that part of us to which we can retreat, if you will, and draw on that spiritual energy that is God. It is there for us to use, but we so often choose to be just human.

In this regard, we are very much like the people of Noah's day, in that we have mixed emotions. Sometimes we think positively, sometimes we can say there's an answer. On the other hand, we sometimes choose to be negative, we choose to be angry, we choose not to trust. We must remember, though, that we operate at both a conscious level and a subconscious level. The subconscious level, which is that feeling nature, picks up the conscious thought; and whatever idea we are working with on a conscious level manifests in our experience. As a result, we sometimes have experiences that cause us to get into a state of consciousness in which we cannot see our way clearly. Let's examine some of these experiences.

SUDDEN AND UNEXPECTED CHANGES

So many times when unexpected events happen, we immediately get upset, we get worried. We don't even wait to see where the answer is going to be. In our anxiety, in our worry, we just assume that we are facing the worst thing that could possibly happen and that there is no way out.

But it is not God's plan that we should worry and be disturbed or anxious about anything. Rather than immediately becoming upset, we need to know how to quiet ourselves and recognize that the change is happening for some purpose in our overall experience.

DELAYS IN HOPED-FOR OCCURRENCES

Sometimes when we are working with an idea, if results don't come when we want them to, we humanly make the decision to "fix it up," to "straighten it out." What we have to learn is that when the outcome or occurrence we are hoping for seems to be delayed, it simply means that there is something in us which is still being worked out so that when the event *does* take place, we will be fully ready and capable of accepting it.

So if the door hasn't opened yet for you, don't shove and push and try to force the lock. Learn to wait, because when a door is to open for you, it will do so automatically; it doesn't require friction. It opens easily, and you step right through and know that this is truly your answer.

Certain Types of Illnesses

We know that there are pathological illnesses (those caused by diseases or tangible substances, such as bacteria) and that there are also psychosomatic illnesses (those whose causes are psychological). I once heard a woman minister make a beautiful statement. She said that when she goes into the hospital, she thinks of it as "the university of life." I took this to mean that irrespective of the illness or its type, even in the hospital room we have the opportunity to go within, to retreat to our indwelling Lord and know the truth that health is already ours. In other words, we can learn from illness.

But if you accept an illness and everything that's said about it as absolute truth—that there's no answer, that the mere name of the illness means certain death—then you are defeating yourself. You have to reach a state of consciousness in which you know that illness does not always mean the end. Even in illness, you still have a loving Father-Mother God with whom you can pray and work. Know that the doctors, the nurses, the technicians, everybody around you is there as an instrument of God. If you can just get your thinking in order, you will know that even in this place you can grow and expand in understanding of God's will for your life.

PERIODS OF BOREDOM

There are so many people who walk around constantly saying, "I'm just bored with life; I'm restless. I don't know what it is, but there's something I'm seeking that I just can't find." What has basically happened in most situations of boredom and restlessness is that you have expended all your energy in one area. Remember that you are a balanced person; you are spirit, mind, and body. But when you expend all your energy in one area of your life, you find you're out of balance.

Some of us put all our energy into our jobs and we never balance ourselves off at a spiritual level. We never really move back to seek guidance and direction. Even our bodies tell us, "I just wish you would stop; I wish you'd let me get some rest!" But we are convinced that there is no alternative, that we have to work long hours to make ends meet. When the body is ready to stop, it is better to stop and give the body the rest than to have it completely collapse on you. If your body collapses, then you'll have a more serious situation than what you had in the first place. You might have money in your pocket, but you can't even enjoy spending it, because the body has just said, "I can't go any further." So when you are experiencing restlessness, when you are experiencing boredom, then you must remember to look at yourself in the light of what you are doing.

WHAT A FLOOD CAN DO FOR YOUR LIFE

Now what am I saying? Simply that all these experiences I've just cited need to be flooded. They need to be flooded with the Spirit. They need to be flooded with an understanding that you don't have to stay in a negative frame of mind. That ark Noah built is symbolic of the ark that you have right inside you. When these kinds of experiences rain down upon you, then you have an ark of safety that you can readily enter and know, as the psalmist said, that *"He that dwelleth in the secret place of the most High shall abide under the shadow of the Almighty"* (Psalm 91:1). And then that flood, that water, becomes a symbol of cleansing in the same way that the flood in Genesis cleansed the earth of the negative thoughts and attitudes of mankind. So when you have negative thoughts, when your attitude gets to the point where you think you can't be what you want to be, *then you need a flood.*

Do I need a flood? *Yes! I need to know that the Spirit of the Lord in me will cleanse me and make me whole if I seek Him. I can seek the Lord through prayer. I can seek the Lord by being quiet. I can seek the Lord by being in a place where there are others who are experiencing this flooding of the Spirit.*

So floods don't have to be detrimental. Floods can be good. If you really want a flood in your life, then right now, right where you are, release the negativity and ask for the flood of the Spirit of the living

God to wash and make you clean so that you can go within your ark of safety and know that all is well. It doesn't matter how devastating it may seem— speak the truth: *The Spirit of God is cleansing and making me whole. I can move the negativity out by speaking words of Truth. I know that the Spirit of the living God is cleansing me and making me whole.*

Oh, how we all need to be flooded, how we all need to know that God is all there is in our lives, that there is nothing else! Call forth a flood in your life, a flood that will do you all the good in the world, because the Spirit of the living God in you is that flooding power that will wash out the negativity in you if you seek Him first in everything. Whether your flood lasts one day or forty days, stick with God; stay with Him; know the Truth. Soon your dove will return to you with the olive branch, the symbol of peace.

CHAPTER TWO

Why Worry
When You Can Pray?

It seems as though we are becoming a nation, a people, of constant worry. When I looked in the dictionary to see what Webster could tell me about worry other than what I already knew, I was reminded that worry means a distressful state of mind. It means anxiety. It means sometimes getting caught up in an experience without seeing an answer for that particular experience.

Recently I was on a plane, flying to another city for a speaking engagement. A very prominent businessman from Chicago sat next to me and we began a conversation. As soon as my seatmate learned that I was a minister, he began telling me about a personal situation that he was going through. In fact, he was on his way home to work out some challenge with his wife. He had been away, and this time of separation was to give them both an opportunity to come back together, to see if they could bring things to a wonderful unity.

Well, we talked for almost an hour. He was clearly seeking my advice, yet each time I responded to him, he'd say, "Yes, but. . . ." This was the tone of the entire conversation. I would suggest the power of prayer, suggest that he turn within and look at himself and then accept his wife as she was. He would respond by saying something like, *"Yes, but* I'm so worried. I really want to work it out, but I'm just worried about what is going to happen before I get home."

Every time I would say something to him that I felt would be helpful, it seemed to frustrate him even more. Eventually I realized that he didn't really want me to help him reach any answer.

Now that's one kind of worry—the kind expressed by people who always say, "Yes, but. . . ." Then there's another kind of worry—that which begins with, "What if. . . ." What if I don't get the job? What if my health fails? What if I don't have enough money?

These are chronic attitudes on the part of many people. All of us have that tendency to want to worry about every little thing. We'd live far more effectively, however, if every time something unsettling happens in this human experience we'd go back to the words of Jesus—back, for instance, to the sixth chapter of Matthew, the thirty-third and thirty-fourth verses. I didn't realize, in fact, until I went back to that passage in preparing this message how much those two verses have meant to me in my life experience:

> But seek ye first the kingdom of God, and His righteousness; and all these things shall be added unto you.
> Take therefore no thought for the morrow; for the morrow shall take thought for the things of itself. Sufficient unto the day is the evil thereof.

However, when we allow ourselves to get into a state of confusion, to get into an attitude of constant worrying, we are really denying that there is a God of righteousness. We are simply saying that there is no answer to whatever the situation is about which we're concerned. But Jesus said, seek the kingdom first. Seek to go within. Seek God in everything. And then you won't have to be so concerned about tomorrow. In other words, *why worry about tomorrow when you can pray today?*

So now we've looked at some of the ways in which we worry—the "Yes, but . . ." and the "What if. . . ." We've defined worry as simply being fearful, afraid that something is or is not going to happen. And we know that fear is the emotion that operates when we don't have faith. Faith in what? Faith in whom? Faith in a presence, faith in an intelligence that is the Creator of this universe. Prayer, then—the other side of the coin of worry—is a conscious act, not something you do haphazardly, but a conscious effort to commune with this Intelligence, this Infinite Spirit that we commonly call God.

We use the word *God* all the time. But we must recognize that God is a force that is everywhere evenly present. We have to remind ourselves over and over again that *God is,* that there is no place where God cannot be found, that God is all-powerful. God is love. God is intelligence. We use these and other attributes to define something that is so great and so wonderful and that operates in so many ways for our highest good that we cannot confine this wondrous Something to a simple definition.

Recognizing, then, that God is everywhere evenly present, we must learn that prayer is simply turning to this Presence in whatever situation we find ourselves. We may not be able to see the Presence, but it becomes apparent whenever we still ourselves. This is what the psalmist meant when he said, *"Be still and know that I am God."* When you still yourself, your anxious thoughts will begin settling. You can put them aside by putting in their place the truth during your time of prayer.

Now I want to share with you some steps in prayer. Let me say first that to pray effectively, you must know that God is the only presence, the only power. When there seems to be something else operating in your life, remember that you are working the law of cause and effect. For every outer experience, there has to be a cause that comes from within you. So begin by recognizing that God is the only presence, the only power.

STEP ONE: PURIFICATION

The first step in effective prayer is to dissolve the worry and purify your mind. That means, among other things, forgiving yourself for having allowed yourself to get entangled and upset because you couldn't face a particular situation for what it was. I don't care what a situation is; you have to face it before you can handle it. And worry simply says, "I don't want to face it."

I know it's easier to say, "I'm so worried . . . I don't see a way . . . I don't see the answer" than it is to face a given situation. If that is the way you initially approached your current challenge, then begin by forgiving yourself for having been at that level of consciousness. That's the purification—cleansing the mind, dissolving those mental blocks of anger, fear, doubt, excuses, self-pity, and blaming of others. Worry has all these things built into it, and you simply must cleanse your mind of them and forgive yourself and anyone else whom you might have held in thoughts of negativity.

STEP TWO: ILLUMINATION

The word *light* appears many times in the Bible. What it's expressing is the need to pray for the expansion and uplifting of your thoughts as you talk to God simply and naturally. Know, too, that you can talk to that Presence just as you would talk to a friend.

You see, when you forgive yourself for feeling foolish and out of place, for fearing that there was no answer, you then begin moving toward the point where you can say, *Father, thank You for illumination. Thank You for light. Thank You for understanding and for showing me how to pray.*

This talking to God is so important. There are many times when I don't know what to say. There's just so much happening in the world that often I'll just get still and I'll say, *God, just feel my mind. Just help me to know how to lift my consciousness, to set my sights on things above. Help me, God, to transform my mind.* That's what Paul meant in Romans 12:2 when he said:

> And be not conformed to this world; but be ye transformed by the renewing of your mind, that ye may prove what is that good, and acceptable, and perfect will of God.

STEP THREE: UNIFICATION

So often when we are praying we don't fully recognize that during this time of prayer we can unify ourselves with God. We can become one with Him, because the minute we still ourselves, the anxiousness has to move out of the way. It is at this moment in which the anxiousness falls away that we begin to feel no separation; then we know that God is not something way off, but that God is right where we are. That Presence is ever available for us to unify ourselves with. This is what Jesus meant when he said, *"I and my Father are one"* (John 10:30). And this same Father is *your* Father.

STEP FOUR: PETITION

Ask God for your desire. You see, the desire is fulfilled through you, through the idea, through the attracting power of God that brings to you all that you need to achieve your goals.

Once you make your petition, once you state your request to the Father, you might, as many people do, experience some doubt whether you're praying for the "right" thing. Here, then, are some questions you can ask yourself to clear up this doubt:

First, *Is what I am praying for good for all concerned? Will having it hurt me or anyone else?*

Second, *Am I willing to give up something that I now have in order to make ready for my new good?* You see, whenever something good comes in, something else moves out. Are you willing for this to happen?

Third, *Am I willing to accept the responsibility for what I am asking?* With fulfilled desires goes the responsibility of making commitments, of making them work for you and following through on them.

If you can answer these questions to your satisfaction, then you can proceed with your prayers with a clean heart and a ready, receptive mind.

STEP FIVE: GRATITUDE

Give thanks for what you have already received. In Matthew 6:32, Jesus tells us that our heavenly Father knows what we have need of even before we ask. What does this mean? It means that the good—whatever it may be—is already there for you. Accept it and give thanks for it.

You may have to begin today with just that act of forgiving yourself for ever having worried in the first place. I've gone through many experiences in life, and I've seen God work. I've seen people without money, and I've seen God bring them what they needed despite their lack of money. For instance, have you ever been without money for food and someone invited you to dinner? That's God! I've seen so many channels open in this way that I *know* that if you will just get into a prayerful attitude and trust that Infinite Intelligence, that Infinite Spirit, God, to work out the perfect plan in your life, a way *will* open where there seemed to be no answer.

I want to suggest something to you that we've often done at Hillside. Take a box—maybe a shoe box, a tissue box, or a box that some small item you bought came in. Call this "God's Thank-You Box" and write on one side of it *Thank You, Father; thank You, Father; thank You, Father. And so it is.* You might also want to add some Scriptures, such as *"And all things, whatsoever ye shall ask in prayer, believing, ye shall receive"* (Matthew 21:22), or *"My God shall supply all your needs according to His riches in glory by Christ Jesus"* (Philippians 4:19). Whatever Scripture you choose, it is simply to remind you that God is the answer, that God is always there. Not a man, not a figure, but a presence, an ever-present help in time of trouble.

Finally, make a little slit in the top of the box and

then put this box in its own special place. Every day, drop in your box a thank-you to God for something, if for no more than for your sense of smell, for your ability to talk. Find something every day for a week that you can thank God for, and place it in your Thank-You Box.

This box is simply a symbol of what God is in your life, an exercise to help you realize how much you are already receiving from the Father. As I say, we've done this at Hillside on occasion, and each time we do it, many people have shared with us afterwards how meaningful it was in reminding them that there are so many things in life, so much about us as children of God, that we can say thank you for.

So I say to you, *Why worry when you can pray?* Take the five steps suggested above and use your Thank-You Box if you need to. You'll find that those worries—whatever they are—can be turned around and transformed. If you are worried about money, say, *Thank You, Father, for the abundance that is mine*. If you are worried about your health, say, *Thank You, Father, for the wholeness that is mine*. If you are worried about how you are going to make it through the next day, say, *Thank You, God, for this day. This is the best day of my life.*

And every time you say, *Thank You,* write out what you're giving thanks for and drop it in your box.

Believe me, this conscious acting out of your prayers will make a difference, because it will serve to remind you to use your power of imagination to know that God is the answer to every situation, your refuge and your strength, a very present help in time of need. Through it all, *why worry when you can pray?*

CHAPTER THREE

When You've Done
All That You Can

*L*et *go and let God.* This saying is a favorite one in the New Thought movement. What it means is that there comes a time when human effort must give over to God effort. It is also directly related to the commandment to remember the sabbath and keep it holy. When we think of the word *sabbath,* we know that it means to rest, to withdraw from all activity. For the Hebrews the number seven was considered a time to rest and to move away from six days of work or continuous activity. Many people, however, tend to feel that the word *sabbath* applies only to Sunday. But if we look at the word's true meaning, then we see that whenever we cease our outer activity and choose instead to rest and to reflect on Spirit or things that are like God, then we are observing a sabbath.

24

This is so true for working people! How many people, for instance, work on the day we call Sunday? If they are religious people and take *sabbath* to mean Sunday, then they might feel that they are sinning because they are at work and not at church. But when the church as an institution has weekday services and weekday activities, then whatever day those who work on Sunday have free—Monday, Tuesday, whatever—they should be able to go to their places of worship and still share in a service activity if they want to observe the sabbath in that sense. So what we're really talking about when we refer to "the sabbath" is the stopping of all the pressures that we're under and the recognition that it's time to really go to the Father.

ANOTHER KIND OF SABBATH

Now this concept of observing the sabbath doesn't apply just to the work you get paid for or to the physical labor or other work you do with your hands. It also applies to the mental work we do in our attempt to solve problems or overcome challenges. These efforts can be every bit as tiring as physical labor, and they too deserve a sabbath.

For instance, suppose you've been working with a problem for some time, or suppose it's a problem that you're facing for the first time. Either way, your first step is to recognize the problem for what it is—a temporary condition that you have the power to control and therefore need not be frightened by.

In the Scriptures, for example, we find the story of Jesus crossing a lake with the disciples after a long day of healing and teaching and working continuously. While they were crossing, a great storm arose, and the disciples became very fearful and woke Jesus up. "Are you just going to let us drown?" they asked him. Well, the first thing Jesus did was to rebuke the waves and tell them to be still, which they did. Then he said to the disciples, *"Why are ye so fearful? How is it that ye have no faith?"* (Mark 4:40).

What does this say to *us*? Many of you right now are going through experiences—you're worrying; some of you have walked the floor all night long. All the walking the floor, all the worrying still has not solved the problem. That worry, that problem, is just like the wind and the waves that frightened the disciples. They put their faith in the winds and the waves and the rolling and the movement. Jesus told them, *Put your faith in a living presence. I'm here. I'm in the boat; and I'm symbolizing the sonship of the One Presence, the One Power, God.*

If you place your faith in that Presence or in Jesus as the representative of it, then you will not be disturbed by the wind and the waves—mental storms, in other words. When unfavorable things are happening to you, the first thing you need to do is recognize that God is all-powerful—the only power in the universe. That's the first thought you have to grasp when in need.

THE STILL, SMALL VOICE

So now you've confronted the problem with a calm mind and you've recognized that God in you gives you the overcoming power. Perhaps you will immediately know of some steps you can take toward working out the problem. Your life experiences and what we call "mother wit" should suggest to you some obvious things that you can do. If you find that you're going to be late with your house payment, for instance, you will of course want to contact your mortgage holder.

But what about this "mother wit" that I speak

of? What is that? In Proverbs, the second chapter, sixth verse, we find these words: *"For the Lord giveth wisdom: out of His mouth cometh knowledge and understanding."* This wisdom is the God-given faculty of intuition; it's what is meant by "the still, small voice of God," which moves through us consciously. When we open ourselves up to listen, to receive, to dwell on the truths of God, then we get within us a flow of thought that is beyond intellect. Intellect is acquired knowledge, knowledge that is learned from teachers, books, newspapers, or any other outside source.

But mother wit, as I say, is the wisdom of God; it's what you feel when you have a "hunch" about something. So if you're still faced with the problem after doing everything you consciously can to solve it, then take a sabbath by getting still in mind and body. No matter how many factors are involved, you'll find that in the stillness, the quietness, a flow of thought will come through your mind. When that flow begins, capture it, hold on to it, and see it as the wisdom of God.

Remember that there is another dimension of you that's greater than your humanness: there's that Spirit of the living God which speaks to your soul,

speaks to your heart all the time, giving you guidance and direction. It is left up to you whether you
will use it. Get still and listen for the answer. It may
not come immediately, but that's why you are taking
a sabbath from the problem. While you are waiting,
all the details are being ironed out; whoever you
have to make contact with is being made ready to see
you; whatever resources you may need are being
made available to you. Thus, you see, the wisdom
of God is constantly working through you so that
when the time comes to act, you'll know *what* to do,
when to do it, and *how* to do it.

One reason we often can't express the wisdom of
God is that we're very fearful. We might think that
others know what's right but that we don't. Many
people, before they decide anything, go and get
everybody's opinion. It's all right to go to people for
advice. But before you do, get still, go to God, and
then to the person that you are directed to go to.
Sometimes off the top of the head, as we say, you
can't think of the right person. But if you take a sabbath at that point—get still, forget about it, go to
lunch, whatever—a name will just flow through your
consciousness when you least expect it. And you'll
know immediately that that's the person for you to

seek out. I have found that when such a name comes through or an idea is revealed to me, it *is* the perfect answer.

Never try to force a solution to a problem, in other words. Every time you get fearful and anxious about what you ought to, take a sabbath. Get still and talk to God. Talk to that Presence, that Power, that Spirit within, which is your teacher. Hold a conversation just as though you were talking with someone face to face. Some people might say you're crazy if you talk to yourself, but don't you believe it! It's good to talk to yourself, to just kind of feel yourself out and get out all the doubt and fear. Don't depend on someone else to decide what is right for you. Accept the recommendations, accept the comments. Then get busy and make a decision based on *your* judgment, and stand by that decision.

ONE DAY AT A TIME

Know that your wisdom faculty operates as good judgment, as discrimination—you can look at things and know whether or not they're good for you; you can make decisions with God's guidance and know that they're the right decisions. Some of us get into trouble financially, emotionally, in our relationships —in so many aspects of our lives—because we try to force solutions, when all we need do is let go and let God. We get in such a hurry! Everything must be done right now, every problem must be solved instantly! But if we would just slow down, take sabbaths when we need them, and recognize that we have a lifetime to do all the things we want to do— then we'd be happy to take life just one day at a time and to take as many sabbaths as we need.

Someone wrote a song called "One Day at a Time, Sweet Jesus," and oh, how true that is! If you'll just take one day, one challenge, and look at it and work with it a little piece at a time, you'll find that wisdom will teach you that when one door closes, another is always ready to open. Instead of being disheartened by closing doors, you'll realize *This has been for my highest good.* When you begin to live in that consciousness, you will be able to look beyond appearances and to avoid panic and unwise decisions. God has built this capacity into you by giving you access to His wisdom and has provided you with a way to reach that wisdom—the sabbath.

Jesus is the perfect example. After so many days of labor, as described at the beginning of this chapter, he did not hesitate to take that period of rest—that's why he and the disciples were crossing the lake: to reach a place where they could rest. He would stop his labor to re-energize, to get back in touch with that living presence called God.

The farmer is another example. He collects the seed, he plants it, he waters it. But the real working of the seed is God. It's God who makes the seed what it was intended to be in the beginning. The sprout, the stem, the leaves—everything that grows does so through the power of Spirit. And this is how it is with our ideas and the solutions to our problems. Whenever you are told to let go and let God, the idea is not that you should just give up, but that you pray about it and let God direct and guide you to right action. Anytime you get to a point where you don't know what to do, stop and take a period of rest.

Making the Sabbath Work for You

Here are some steps for taking an effective sabbath and developing your wisdom faculty:

1. *Have periods of meditation and prayer.* Begin your day by taking at least fifteen minutes to listen, to just get still. If you have to start with five minutes and work your way up to fifteen, it's okay. Find a technique to help you attain this stillness. It may be beautiful music or may be poetry; it may be the Scriptures. Whatever it is, take time to meditate on something that is beautiful and that will lift your consciousness above what you know you'll be facing during the day. While you're in this meditative state, speak the truth. Say, *God, you are in control of my day. I give it over to You so that Your wisdom will come through me in everything I do.* Then repeat this period of meditation at midday and at night.

2. *Listen for inspiration from Spirit.* The Scriptures say, *"Be still and know that I am God."* I just went on a trip, for instance, and so many ideas came flowing through my mind because I took time to listen for them.

3. *Let your mind dwell on the qualities of God.* What are those qualities? Love, sharing, giving, understanding, patience, tolerance—all the qualities that we love when we see them in other people. As

the apostle Paul said, *"Whatsoever things are true, whatsoever things are honest, whatsoever things are just, whatsoever things are pure, whatsoever things are lovely, whatsoever things are of good report . . . think on these things"* (Philippians 4:8). Those are the qualities of God.

4. *Act on the inspiration received.* When you receive the inspiration, don't just hold it and not use it. Maybe you and your co-workers have been wrestling with something technical and suddenly you get a flow of thought. Act on it, because it comes straight from the one Source: God the Good omnipotent.

Whatever problem you're facing, do the best that you can do toward solving it. Then don't be afraid to take a sabbath—let go and let God. Somewhere along the line, the consciousness of opposition—whether within you or without—will give way in your favor.

CHAPTER FOUR

After the Divorce, Then What?

We hear so much today about the high divorce rate in this country. We generally use the word *divorce* to mean the dissolution of a marriage. In the broader sense of the word, however, we sometimes are divorced from *ourselves* because we really don't know the true self of us. Sometimes people are divorced from their jobs, from their families, from their environment, just sort of functioning at a level of thinking that they don't need anything or anybody else. This causes them to separate themselves out.

But I want to look particularly at divorce as it relates to marriage, and I want to use the Bible reference Matthew 19:6, in which Jesus says, *"What therefore God hath joined together, let not man put asunder.''* In this particular chapter, Jesus was explaining to the people about their misuse of the bill of divorcement given to them during Moses' time. All it took then was for a man to say three times to his wife, ''I divorce you,'' and it was over. Jesus, then, was rebuking them for their attitude that they could just run away from situations rather than work through them.

At one time I seemed to have a lot of men coming to me for counseling about divorces. I remember one young man in particular who shared his experience with me. He had married and moved his wife here from another city; but after having been here for six months, his wife was unhappy and didn't like the city. For any number of reasons she had decided that she didn't want to be married; she wanted a divorce, she wanted to go back to her family and to the city from which she came. This young man was in his early thirties, making a good living, traveling all over the world. He just couldn't understand how his marriage could be falling apart after such a short time. And to make it worse, he and his wife couldn't talk about the situation.

This wasn't his first marriage. Fresh out of high school, he had married his childhood sweetheart and thought it the zenith of his life. That marriage didn't last long, either—no more than a couple of years. They both explained the failure of that marriage by saying that they were too young. Now, at the age of thirty-three, he was facing his second divorce.

As I talked to this young man and began to understand what had led him into his two marriages, it occurred to me that we would all be so much better off if our peers, parents, friends, and acquaintances whom we respect would encourage premarital counseling, rather than routinely expecting everyone to get married. In our society there seems to be a bias that people who aren't married are strange animals. But with proper counseling, many people might find that for whatever reasons, they don't actually need to be married at all. Think how many divorces *that* would prevent!

WHAT ARE WE EXPECTING FROM MARRIAGE, ANYWAY?

Let me stop for a moment and share what I think is an excellent definition of marriage by Eric Butterworth, one of the most respected writers in the New Thought movement: *Marriage is the license by which two people who have seen the greater possibilities in each other may work together to bring forth those possibilities. It is a laboratory of individual unfoldment.* In a marriage, then, two people ought to be able to see beyond the image they project and see the good behind the image. They ought to see and accept each other as individuals who have come together to work at something worthwhile and to bring their good into a happy, loving union.

By contrast, we ministers too often feel that when we conduct a wedding ceremony, it seals the marriage. But the ceremony does not seal the *attitude,* it does not seal the *consciousness* that two people must have when they join in marriage. For the marriage to be successful, the couple must bring to it an attitude of working together toward understanding and supporting each other, not just a casual, "Well, we're married now, so we must be in love!"

And this suggests two other problems which often keep marriages from being successful: the misunderstanding of the word *love,* and the idea that someone can *make* us happy. As for our misinterpretation of the word *love,* what we need to understand is that one can't just marry and expect the mate to provide love automatically. The love has to flow *within* each of us; it must be activated internally, so to speak, before it can be felt. And as for the idea of others bringing us happiness, about all that another person can really do is help you enjoy what happiness you already possess. You've got to know before you get married that you can be happy with yourself. Then when you meet someone else who also knows this self-happiness, the two of you come together and your happiness is reflected in each of you. In other words, love comes *from* you; love meets love in another individual; love binds itself to more love and becomes a beautiful experience.

You Must Take Responsibility for Yourself

To the young man who had come to me seeking counseling, I said, "All right, so here you are with two marriages that ended in divorce. What are you doing about *yourself* now? Have you really stopped and looked at yourself to see if you feel good about yourself? You may be seeking happiness from someone else or from some outside object, when what you need to do is learn to build some happiness within you."

What am I talking about? *Self-esteem.* This simply means what we think or feel about ourselves, what kinds of attitudes we have built up over a period of years based on what others say, what others have told us about ourselves and how they have encouraged us to think about ourselves. Many "bad" marriages are the product of one party or the other lacking self-esteem and therefore seeking to ease the pain and reach a desired psychological level by relying on someone else. This doesn't work.

I told this to my counselee and said that before he made another step, he had to begin working with himself. First, he had to reconnect himself with his spiritual self. He answered that besides going to his own weddings, he really hadn't been to church. "But more than going to church," I said, "how do you feel about your love of God? About just knowing that there's something greater within you that you can hold on to, that you can know will be there?"

The Scriptures, after all, tell us that there is a Spirit in man and that the inspiration of that Spirit gives us understanding. The extent to which we stir up that Spirit is an expression of the way we feel about ourselves.

I assured the young man that I wasn't blaming him for the divorce—there are always two sides, and some people say three sides. The important thing to remember, though, is that divorce is not the end. From there, you can begin to work with yourself, to pick up the pieces. Every day you get up, seek that inner guidance, direction, and you will begin to know that you are a person, that nobody and no thing can keep your good from you.

Remember, life is filled with change, and every time you go through a change, it's part of your own personal growth and development. We go from classroom to classroom. Each experience you have can strengthen you if you will see it as an opportunity to look at how well you're functioning. As I said, one can be divorced from anything—including God. Some of us don't even know that we are perfect, whole children of God. We just kind of move through the universe at our own rate of speed, and suddenly it takes an experience like a divorce to help us see what we ought to be about. So if you've recently gone through a divorce, don't throw up your hands, don't get angry, don't hold hate or resentment, don't try for the "payback." But stop and realize that this experience has come into your life for your soul growth. You drew this experience to yourself because you drew a particular person into your life.

Maybe you ran too fast. Maybe you didn't even

try to discuss what you ought to have done about it. Maybe you didn't go for counseling; maybe you didn't seek the Lord; maybe you didn't seek guidance. If that's the way it was, then accept it and say, "It's all right." Then ask yourself, "Where do I go from here? How do I pick up the pieces and begin getting myself in Divine order so I can live to the fullest, so I can know that after the divorce I can still be a total person?" Here are some steps that may help you:

1. *Reconnect yourself with your Divine Source.* Recognize that there is a Spirit in you, that God has helped you to get through the pain and the hurt. Just take the Lord's Prayer and you will know that you don't have to hold any animosity or thoughts of getting even. When you learn to release a person to his or her own highest good, then you can stand on your own two feet and be what you ought to be and know that that person is no longer a part of your life. In other words, in releasing you can begin moving to your own highest good.

That's why Jesus said, "What *God* hath joined together." The problem is that many times God has not been in the midst of our marital situations, because we're just functioning at a human level. But if you now find yourself in a divorce experience, first of all recognize that there is a presence, there is a power—God the Good omnipotent—that you can turn to and ask for guidance. As I said to the counselee, go back and look at your faith and trust. See what you can build on. Let's not forget that no matter how successful we are in our careers and other outer endeavors, it's God within us that helps us to be the successes we are. When you turn on a light-switch, the electricity is always there. But until you turn the switch on, you'll never have the light. So it is with the ever-present God.

2. *Forgive your former mate as you forgive yourself.* It makes no sense to harbor feelings of guilt, resentment, or bitterness at a time like this. The legal and physical details of breaking up a household and the emotional trauma are enough to deal with. Why add unnecessary hard feelings to the burden?

You don't know what will come from the experience, but at least give yourself a forgiveness treatment. If you don't forgive, all the anger and resentment will affect you, because whatever you're feeling toward someone else affects you first. In affecting you, it affects your job, your relationships with other people, and every aspect of your life.

3. *Remind yourself that there is a lesson in this for your good.* Then thank God for the opportunity to learn the lesson. Regardless of what happens in any life experience, you can pick up the pieces, mend them with the help of God, and keep moving. You need not stop. God in you will carry you through any situation.

GOD YESTERDAY, GOD TODAY, GOD TOMORROW

Once you begin to love yourself again and the God within, you will attract a person who also is experiencing that same love of God. Then you can begin a new relationship, work at it, and know that you can see it through. If that person does not come into your experience, don't worry about it. Just involve yourself in your church, involve yourself in various activities, in volunteer work perhaps—whatever will help you build a positive mental attitude and be the child of God you were meant to be. And if the right person *does* come along and you choose not to marry again, that's all right too.

Affirm for yourself: *Changes may come in my life; but God in me is the yesterday, today, and to-morrow.* No matter what it is, no matter what you're going through, you don't have to feel sorry for yourself. Instead, direct your attention to the Presence within you; speak words that will build up rather than tear down; release the other person and know that in releasing, you gain your own sense of stability. Continue to put the light of God around yourself and the situation.

Yes, divorce can be painful. But if you'll just touch that Spirit in you, you'll find that God allows us to make a come-back even from our most painful mistakes. Just be happy and mindful that God in you is a God of love and peace. We are always under grace through Christ Jesus, so hold on just a little longer.

CHAPTER FIVE

In the Stillness
Is Strength

From time to time we all face situations that we'd rather not have to deal with. Perhaps a difficult meeting awaits us at work, or there might be a painful conflict at home that simply must be worked out. Or the challenge may be something internal, such as a difficult decision or trying to overcome fear, doubt, illness, a damaging habit. Whatever the situation, our human resources alone may not be sufficient for handling it. At such times, what a blessing it is to know that we are endowed with certain faculties of mind that we can use to keep ourselves in tune, in contact with the Christ consciousness.

We can be renewed and transformed in mind and in body, for instance, when we call forth the faculty of strength. This is one of the twelve faculties of man as revealed to Charles Fillmore, co-founder of the

Unity movement. In a vision, Mr. Fillmore was shown that the twelve apostles of Jesus represent twelve spiritual powers in each of us. And just as Jesus called forth the twelve apostles to train them and to teach them his message so that they could then go out into the world and preach the gospel, heal the sick, raise the dead—in the same way, we know that such powers are available to us today.

When we talk about the faculty of strength, most people think of power, of being a great might. But strength is also expressed on the spiritual level, and it must first be in that respect that you understand strength. There is no power, there is no might, there can be no physical expression unless one understands the inner foundations of his or her strength. You already have built right into your soul the strength that you need. As within, so without. Therefore, what you have to do is draw from the inner in order to produce the kind of outer experience that you want.

There are certain easy-to-learn steps that will help you master the technique of turning within for strength. The first thing you'll have to do is regain control of your thoughts and reactions to the threatening situation. Have you ever heard someone say, "I feel like I just want to cry. If I could, I know I'd feel so much better." Well, if you ever feel that way, then go ahead and have a good cry. Often, day-to-day tension and frustration cause us to react on an emotional level. When you get into that level of consciousness where crying seems like the only release, then it just may be the best thing for you. Crying, you see, is a form of releasing anxiety; and when you are crying, you begin to leave behind the tension and the feelings of defeat and depression. Not until you accomplish this can you begin to feed your conscious mind with thoughts of strength.

When you release tension and feelings of defeat, there is that in you which begins to pick up; and somehow you just know that it's going to be all right. Philippians 4:13 tells us that *"I can do all things through Christ which strengtheneth me."* So just by speaking and truly believing words of truth, you begin to have the lifting up from that level of not knowing which way you're going. But in order to do this, you have to still yourself. The key to all of this is, *"Be still and know that I am God."* Become still so that you can still feel and know that inner strength, that strength of God which passeth all understanding

First Relax

Often, we try to call up our strength when we are upset or irritated about something. If that is the case, you might want to withdraw to a quiet place so that you can come down off that anger and irritability. In your quiet location, sit in a relaxed way and feel yourself breathing the breath of God. Remember, breath is life, and life is God. If you've been under a lot of pressure, just feel yourself relaxing in body. Maybe you're having a challenge with a particular part of your body. Remember, you can speak the word of strength to that part of your body. Know that your words have the power to lift you up.

After you've relaxed your body, close your eyes for a moment and speak the truth with this affirmation: *I still myself toward Divine strength.* In this time of quiet, recognize that there is only one power, one presence, God the Good. That God is the strength of your being. If while doing this relaxation exercise you have the tendency to drop off and go to sleep, that's all right, because in that quietness and time of rest comes the strength to do what you have to do upon awakening.

Complete your relaxation exercise by declaring to yourself, *I feel myself full of Divine strength.* The lifting in consciousness that you will feel at this point is also raising your body and your affairs to Divine order.

SEE YOURSELF IN A DIFFERENT LIGHT

Most of us don't have very much patience with ourselves. That's why we are so likely to go out and buy the "extra-strength pain reliever" we see advertised. But once the physical pain has passed off, there is still the psychological or emotional pain to deal with. The problem is still there, because we haven't learned to recognize that we have the power of that inner strength to see it through and to find an answer. But when you get in the habit of stilling yourself, you find that you have a great deal of patience.

You might also find that you are more tolerant of others than you thought you were. So often we are unfair to ourselves and to others because we can't tolerate people's differences. Sometimes we're not tolerant because someone doesn't belong to our religious denomination; because someone doesn't accept what we think is the greatest idea in the world; because someone has different values from the ones we hold. Whatever the differences, what we have to realize is that each person has the right to operate at his own level of awareness. So if tolerance is a stumbling block for you, try telling yourself, "Even though I disagree with this person, I can at least listen to what he's saying and be open to it and then proceed to work toward a solution in the way that's best for my experience." You never know how you might be blessed, what you might learn just from the simple act of listening with an open mind, knowing all the while that *you* can make up your own mind.

FINALLY, PRAY IN CONFIDENCE AND IN FAITH

Having stilled and relaxed yourself and gained a bit of patience, you are now ready to take action toward solving the problem that confronts you. Out of strength we learn to pray in faith, believing that our prayers will be answered in the way that's best for our particular situation. Can you imagine what will begin to happen in your life not only when you have faith in God and believe that all things are possible, but when you also rely on the strength of God to bring your prayer into manifestation? So many of us pray in a negative fashion; we pray as if God didn't love us. But God *does* love us. It is not the Father's will that any of his children should perish or suffer. So we can go to God, as Jesus said, and act as if what we're praying for were already done. And when you get an intuitive thought at the end of your prayer, that is the Father saying, "This is your next step."

Then you go back and say, "Thank You, God, for the courage to follow through on what You've given me to do." That's the strength, the flow that is there for you to draw upon every moment of the day.

What all this means is that prayer is the key to recognizing that the strength of God is present in you to guide you, to give you the courage to do what you have to do. When we learn to spend time every day in the quiet with our Father-Mother God, it makes such a difference in our lives! If you've been working hard all week and feel heavy, tired, as though you couldn't go one step farther, just get still right where you are and recognize that God is the strength of your being. God is the expression through you of love, of wisdom, and of understanding.

CHAPTER SIX

Is Wealth
for a Select Few?
(Part 1)

In recent times we seem to be surrounded by a consciousness that insists that there isn't enough to go around, that there'll be nothing for future generations but suffering and preparation for war. So much of this negative emotion has found its way into the universe that I want to reassure you, as I have been reassuring myself, that a loving Father-Mother God will not deny His children goodness when the children come back to·Him, as did the prodigal son. To begin with, we must learn to listen to the inner guidance, the intuition, the still, small voice of God in whatever we do, whether it's in our church, in our homes, in our offices or other work sites.

But today, history is repeating itself. We're talking about inflation. Everybody's concerned. I've been speaking at colleges and high schools, and I pick up a fearful attitude on the part of students who are afraid of what their future holds in the face of proposed federal cutbacks in educational funds. They're afraid that they will not have an opportunity to make it through school because doors will be closed to them.

Even so, when I answer the question "Is wealth for a select few?" I have to say, "No!" The problem is simply that we have gotten so caught up in the physical aspects of living that we've forgotten that there is another dimension waiting for us to use in all its power and glory to move into our lives the goodness we were created to have. We were created out of love. We were created to have the goodness of our Creator. And the Scriptures tell us that the Father knows what we have need of even before we ask.

The question then becomes, Who are we asking? Who are we looking to for our financial needs? Who are we seeing as the source? I believe with all my heart, soul, and mind that there is only one source, and that's God. I believe that God as Spirit, as an Infinite Intelligence, works with us through our conscious thinking. Remember, whatever we are conscious of is what we experience in our daily lives.

We think and act and feel based on what our human intelligence tells us. But we must also be bathed with the Spirit of God; and this means we must know how to speak and think truth. There are many instances in the Scriptures where men and women were "up against it," so to speak, and knew of no way out. But they always seemed to find their way back to that other dimension, that spiritual self, that God self, and to recognize that they could do nothing of themselves; but with God, all things were possible to them.

I love the words Jesus spoke in Matthew, the sixth chapter, verses thirty through thirty-four:

> Wherefore, if God so clothe the grass of the field, which today is, and tomorrow is cast into the oven, shall he not much more clothe you, O ye of little faith?
>
> Therefore take no thought, saying, What shall we eat? or, What shall we drink? or, Wherewithal shall we be clothed?

(For after all these things do the Gentiles seek:)
for your heavenly Father knoweth that ye have
need of all these things.

But seek ye first the kingdom of God, and his
righteousness; and all these things shall be added
unto you.

Take therefore no thought for the morrow; for
the morrow shall take thought for the things of
itself. Sufficient unto the day is the evil thereof.

WHERE ARE YOU "COMING FROM"?

I believe that wherever you are today in your awareness of how your financial needs can be met, it has
to do with childhood influences. Some of us came
from an environment in which we had plenty. Others
came out of environments where all they had was
anger and resentment and envy and criticism and
lack.

So many of us have come from backgrounds that
we label negatively. And when we label people, they
take those labels and come to believe very strongly
that they can't be anything but what they've been
labeled. That's where the breakthrough has to

come—to help a person know that it is not the label but one's attitude that counts. You must have faith to believe that no matter what the conditions are, if you can keep yourself in tune with Spirit and believe that a way will be made, then *it will be so.*

I, for instance, came out of an environment that might be labeled a "poor" one. But I was raised by my grandmother, who knew that there was something beyond the human. She always looked to that spiritual self for guidance and direction. I remember times when my grandmother would cut out pasteboard and put it in my shoes when they were worn thin and she didn't have the money to have them half-soled. What she was doing was taking what she had and using it. That idea had to come from someplace. Deep within her, she wanted me to go to school. She did not want my feet to touch the ground, yet she had no money. So God, that Infinite Intelligence, worked through her mind and gave her the idea; and therefore I never had to miss a day of school.

And throughout the years of my upbringing by my grandmother, in the words that she spoke to me I never heard the word *poor.* And things were meager there. I can remember a pot-bellied stove and having to "split a chunk," as we called it, and breaking up kindling to make a fire for that stove. Nevertheless, I was taught to be thankful and to know that if I thanked God for what I was receiving, more would come.

Now from that very modest beginning to this present time, I have seen God's spiritual laws work. I know what it means to work your way through school. I worked my way through as a bus girl, dishwasher, and maid—not what one would consider "status" positions. But in everything, I learned to be thankful for the opportunity to grow spiritually, mentally, and emotionally.

I wish I had kept a diary or journal of every door that opened for me when I had thought there was no way. I wish I had written down the exact feelings I had when a door opened for me during my second year at Texas Southern University, when I had no tuition money the day school began and somebody let me register anyhow! God always works through some channel to open a door. But it is your conscious awareness, it is your belief, your thought that you use to connect yourself to this power called God.

Labels! I'd never heard the word *ghetto* until I got to graduate school. Didn't know a thing about it. But it doesn't matter whether it's called *ghetto* or something else. You have to rise above it in your thinking. Look at it and decide that you can survive it and make it work for you.

USE YOUR INNER RESOURCES

The first thing you have to be aware of is that there is a presence and a power that works through you when you allow it to. We have to learn that what we are looking for is right inside us. If we just listen, we'll find that we have so much to work with. You can start in a one-room apartment; you can start in five rooms. But wherever you are, look around you and begin to see what's there for you to use.

We need to retrain our thinking. We need to look at our beginnings only long enough to recognize that no matter what we have come through, it's okay. When you recognize that you can use your experiences to step on as though they were stones across a creek, then you realize it doesn't matter what your background is.

How can we open ourselves through the retraining of our minds and come to understand that prosperity is ours? Well, there's a perfectly logical process involved.

1. *You have to know that you don't depend on persons or conditions for your prosperity.* You bless persons, you bless conditions as channels; but God is the source of your supply. God provides his own amazing channels of supply to you right now. But if you depend on the boss, if you depend on the paycheck—suppose the paycheck doesn't come? Then what do you do? There has to be another channel. You have to learn not to give up if one door closes, not to throw up your hands. Instead, seek another idea from God; wait for it to come and then move on with it.

2. *You have to let go of worn-out things, worn-out conditions, worn-out relationships.* Sometimes we get caught up with ideas and conditions. Inflation is one such idea. You have to release that kind of thinking from your mind and move away from relationships and people who reinforce it. Move

away from people who constantly say that there is no answer.

3. *The act of release that I just mentioned is magnetic.* Through releasing, you draw to you that which is yours. Let go and grow! Let go of the negative thinking. Let go of the impossibility thoughts that say there's no solution.

4. *You must forgive all that has offended you, within and without.* Things past, things present, things future, you must forgive. You must forgive everything and everybody who could *possibly* need forgiveness.

Sometimes we are blocked from receiving our good because we have so much anger. We're resentful of our supervisor; we're resentful of people we work with; we're resentful of our former mates. You have to stop that kind of thinking and realize that in forgiving yourself, you open up a flow of ideas that will lead you to know what to do. Forgiveness is an inner act. It's releasing a negative emotion about somebody or something. Many think that they can't get a raise on their job or fear that they're going to be laid off. You have got to forgive that whole situation and know that if that door closes, then certainly you have a gift from God, a talent that you can use elsewhere. And when you realize that fact, you can stop looking to use your gift in the same place you just left. You see, it doesn't matter. You can start where you are; you can learn to use what you have.

5. *Do the work you love, and love the work you do.* When you love something, it draws to you more opportunities to express yourself in the area that brings you pleasure.

WEALTH IS FOR YOU

Wealth is *not* for a select few, because wealth means "well-being." Whether it's wealth of mind, wealth of health, wealth of material goods—no matter what the goodness that you desire, know that God did not design this world so there would always be the haves and the have-nots. *Man* has structured that. But those of us who believe must use our spiritual self and stand on the promises of God and know that doors will open for us. Know where you want to go.

Don't give up; set your goals and picture what you want to do. See yourself making it step by step.

Most of all, remember that your heavenly Father knows what you have need of before you ask. Learn to still your anxious thoughts. Look at the flowers. Even with the changing of the seasons, they have a natural flow. And if you will just learn to move with that same flow, the flow of God, you will know that your good is at hand. Take your mind off your anxieties for a few moments and just say:

God, I'm Yours. You created me out of Yourself, and I believe that Your will for me is all good. Wherever my financial need may be expressing itself, I know that with You all things are possible. I thank You right now for every channel, every door that opens. I'm coming back to You, knowing that You will cleanse and feed my mind and bathe me in Your Spirit until I know that there's an answer, there's an answer, there's an answer. And I accept that answer right now. Through the Christ within, thank You, Father; thank You, Father; thank You, Father. And so it is!

CHAPTER SEVEN

Is Wealth
for a Select Few?
(Part 2)

I've already answered this question in the preceding chapter. No, wealth is *not* for the select few! Wealth is God's gift to His children and, as such, is for everyone who will take the time to understand and apply its laws. But since so many of us have been conditioned to believe that we cannot be prosperous, this is a topic that people never seem to hear enough about. So let's continue the discussion.

At Hillside we define prosperity as peace of mind, health, wealth, and the entire joy of living. But often at the mention of prosperity, people think only of money. Yet there are any number of people in the universe who have lots of money but don't have good health. So you see, we're talking about a complete-ness, a wholeness of understanding that God is the source of every good thing there is in the universe.

What constantly amazes me is the extent to which we separate our religion from everything else. We use our minds to get ideas for our jobs, ideas for our homes, ideas for the governing of our country. We use those ideas; but we cannot comprehend that the same mind is fertile soil for ideas that relate to the promises of God concerning prosperity. Yet if we plant God's truths about prosperity in our minds, we will reap the benefits just as we do with other concerns that we have.

I did social work for years, for example. We used to have various activities for children, youth, and adults; and I would sit in my office and work up ideas and plans for various kinds of programs. Soon I got to be known as a good "idea person." I didn't know then as I do now that those ideas had come from God; but it was as I expanded in the use of those ideas and involved other people that I began to move up the ladder in my career and to achieve financial success. Step by step, every one of my pro-motions came as a result of my learning to use those ideas. Not until much later did I understand that that's how God brings our good through us—by speaking to us through that flow of thought.

If you think of your mind as fertile soil, then the thoughts that you place in your mind are the seeds that go in the soil. Would it not be just as beneficial if we could plant a positive seed of truth? If you will plant in your mind *My God shall supply all my needs according to His riches and glory*—plant that seed and nurture it with the belief that you don't have to go around crying the blues and complaining all the time about what you *don't* have, what you *can't* get—you will find that when you replace those negative thoughts with this positive seed, then you will have an excitement, an expectation, a knowingness that things, positions, and challenges are going to be resolved in your favor. Whether it relates to a romance, a relationship with your family, your job, going to school, buying furniture—whatever: when you know that Spirit is there to guide you, you will then go within more, get still, and speak to that Presence.

What most of us haven't realized is that when we pray about an issue and an idea comes through our consciousness, it's God responding to us, because our minds are our connecting link with the Infinite Intelligence that pervades this entire universe. So look only to God; look only to Spirit. Learn to stop, take time, say, "What do I do next? What is my answer?" Then have the patience to let it flow, because you'll get an answer.

TAKE A LESSON FROM THE ISRAELITES

Throughout the years, a very popular book among Hillsiders has been Georgiana Tree West's *Prosperity's Ten Commandments,* which is based on the ten commandments as given to Moses by God. Years ago I saw the movie *The Ten Commandments,* and one of the things that impressed me most about it was that when Moses was receiving the commandments, there was not a physical body there. The commandments were being hurled like fire through the universe right onto the tablets of stone. Of course that was a Hollywood production, but still it takes us back to the idea that Jesus gave us, namely that God is Spirit. This is an example of Spirit zooming through the mind of man to give man the ideas that It wants revealed to Its people.

Remember that Moses was leading a rebellious

people, a people who had just been freed from
Egypt. They had to have some laws—and the name
"Moses," by the way, means *law*. They needed
moral and spiritual laws to live by in order to get
along with each other, but more importantly, for
relating to their Creator.

Let's look at the first commandment God gave
Moses (Exodus 20:3):

Thou shalt have no other gods before me.

Coming out of Egypt, a land filled with the worship of idol gods, the Israelites obviously needed this
commandment first. Notice that the word gods in
the Scripture begins with a small *g*—not a capital
g—indicating that it applied to the little gods that we
hold to, accept, believe in, and place before the
power and the might of an ever-present Spirit that
is so real in our lives. Some of these little gods are
doubt, worry, fear, anger—in other words we get
caught up in the world and what it's all about.

As long as you dwell on the small gods, they will
keep you from touching the real God, the real Intelligence, the real Power. By dwelling on these little
gods, you get caught up in the human element. Now
this does not mean that there is not supposed to be

a human element. But I feel that it's a part of our growth to realize that the human element has the opportunity to be spiritualized as we acknowledge that there is a Divine Presence in this universe that is the constant provider of all our needs.

Don't accept the little gods, because they are what causes us to have negative outer experiences. If you're fearful about something, you might just bring it into your life by dwelling on it. Instead, turn within and recognize the power there. Remember, the opposite of fear is faith.

What thoughts have you accepted as your little gods? What can you do about them? Take this affirmation: *I look only to God for my supply.* Recognize that God as the spiritual substance of the universe has supplied all you need. And you pick up that supply by the words you speak and the thoughts you think. What are you thinking right now? Are you thinking fear? Doubt? Worry? Then remember: *I look only to God for my supply. I will have no other god before Him. There is only one Presence, there is only one Power: God the Good omnipotent.*

Taking this commandment one step further, remember that there is only one *source* in our lives and that source is the wisdom, the power, the love, the intelligence of God. The way we contact this source is to speak the truth, hear the truth, expect the truth. We can do that by means of our daily prayer time, we can do that by filling our consciousness with inspirational material. This will keep us mindful that there is only one presence, one power in the universe.

This realization will lift us above the consciousness of lack. You know, we read so much in the papers about shortages here, shortages there; about budget deficits; about cutbacks. Well, let me tell you one thing: God is still the source. There is no one man in this country, no five men, no group of men that can stop God from being the source. Cutbacks may come and cutbacks may go. But there will always be plenty to share and plenty to spare as long as God's people realize this truth. We must go back to the idea that God is the source and the everprovider.

KEEP THE DOOR OPEN FOR PROSPERITY

Are you in the habit of using limiting words? Some of us say all the time, "I'm down to my last dime

. . . I don't know how I'm going to manage. . . . How am I going to pay my rent next month?'' Why worry about next month if you can't handle this one? Jesus said, *"Sufficient unto the day is the evil thereof"* (Matthew 6:34). It's enough of a task, in other words, just to get through this day. And when you speak limiting words such as these, all you're doing is giving power to them. Before you know it, they're part of your living experience.

Another way we close the door on prosperity is by talking down success—saying, for instance, that we're spending or making too much money. So many of us, when things are opening up for us, can't seem to accept it. ''I can't believe this is happening to me!'' As a result, we kind of berate ourselves. We don't think we deserve the best.

Remember the idea of the seed and your fertile mind? Well, that fertile mind, that soil of your subconscious mind, accepts positive *and* negative seeds. It can't tell the difference—a seed is a seed. So what do you suppose happens when you berate yourself over your spending habits? That's right! You create in your subconscious mind the idea that you're not *supposed* to have or enjoy prosperity, that you don't *deserve* it. Then, sooner or later, that very same subconscious mind, which you've inflicted all that guilt on, will find a way to relieve you of some of those guilt feelings by leading you to create conditions that will move your prosperity right out of your experience!

Finally, don't close the door on your prosperity by misusing it. Have you ever been on a shopping spree? We get in the store and get carried away by all the beautiful displays and just *love* everything we buy. And that's wonderful—God's riches were put here for us to enjoy, not merely to long for. But oh, do we cuss and fuss when it comes time to pay the bills! Remember, the stores honored you by letting you come and buy on credit. You have the same responsibility to honor the store by paying the bill and paying it lovingly.

I say all the time, when you pay those bills, hold them in your hands before you release them and thank God that you have the opportunity to pay them. And thank Him again because you know that you will continue to have that flow of money substance, that flow of everything to meet your needs.

And be sure that you deal honorably with God.
When God provides you, through your job, through
any channel, a way to meet your obligations, go and
pay your bills. A lot of people have money and won't
even use it to pay their debts. When you do this, you
are not being honorable with God. God has provided for you, so pay your bills instead of going out
and throwing money away or squandering it. When
God opens a channel for you and provides the money
you need to pay bills, know that you have a particular obligation to use that money for the purpose God
provided it for. See the parable of the talents (Matthew 25:14–30) for a lesson on the responsible handling of money.

IT'S UP TO YOU

So nobody has to miss out on prosperity. Nobody has
to be unsuccessful. It depends on us to work the law
of cause and effect. Put out your best; expect the best.
Remember that God is the source of your supply.

And I might tell you this also: begin by forgiving yourself for even the slightest thought you had

that you were limited, that you couldn't make it. Expand with each experience and keep believing that you too have your rightful place in God's plan. The choice is to believe that you can't make it or to believe that with God's help you can. The more you put God's truth as seeds into the fertile soil of your mind, the more you will believe and the more you will see it in your outer experience.

There are many channels, many paymasters. But God is the ultimate reality, the source of it all.

CHAPTER EIGHT

You Are Not Alone

In every best-seller on emotions or psychological concerns, there's a chapter on how to overcome loneliness. In some of these books there is the misconception that women are lonelier than men. But studies have indicated that men and women experience loneliness about equally. Men may not talk of loneliness as much as women do, but it is the same challenge for both male and female.

In coping with loneliness, we must first go back to the truth that life is consciousness. What is consciousness? It's awareness. Whatever you are aware of is what you will express in your everyday life. Also, loneliness is a state of mind that we accept for ourselves as a fact or truth of our being. But if you look at the whole idea of loneliness, you will find that it had to be first just that—an idea in your mind. If you keep that idea and reinforce it—''I'm lonely,'' or ''I don't have anybody,'' or ''I have no friends''—then you begin to breathe life into that state of mind and eventually you will feel it subconsciously where your emotions are. This leads to feelings of rejection, alienation, and generally a sense that life has dealt you a rough blow.

BE HONEST WITH YOURSELF

Before you can break the grip of loneliness, you have to work with your feelings about yourself. As long as you accept the idea of loneliness in your life, it will control and keep you in this frame of mind. Look at yourself as a person and ask yourself, ''What has caused me to get in the state of consciousness to believe that there's nobody around but me? Why do I reject others? Why do I feel that others have rejected me and that I have no friends?'' In other words, the first step is just being honest with yourself.

This was Jesus' message all the time. He was constantly teaching us how to look at ourselves and see what we are, what we need, what we have to do about a particular situation. That's still the biggest challenge we have today. We really don't take time to look at the situation we're in and to work with it honestly.

Recognize, then, that if you're going to think in terms of loneliness, then you are accepting it and really not participating in the beautiful life-stream around you. So the first step is to look at yourself and see what got you to the point of rejection, alienation, friendlessness. When you can face the answers to these questions, that is the first step. Psychologists have found that people who are lonely in their old age were lonely when they were younger. We sort of get into a box and accept loneliness, telling ourselves that there's nothing that can be done about it. But if you don't like the way your life is going, if you don't want it to be this way for years to come, then you must begin *now* to take responsibility for it.

YOUR WORK CAN WORK FOR YOU

Second, what is your occupation? Are you happy in it? Is it fulfilling? Do you really get excited about going to work? Some people get up and pray about getting through Monday. By Friday, they're happy because the weekend is coming. But then here comes Monday again. What a vicious circle! On Fridays they're excited, the work week is over. Come Monday, they're falling apart again.

Re-examine your occupation. See what it means to you. Is it an excitement? Do you enjoy doing what you do? As you begin to move into areas of work that are enjoyable, you attract to you people who enjoy their work just as you do. That could be the beginning of a good, positive relationship.

Perhaps you're not working. Maybe you're retired or at home for some other reason. If so, look at the time of day that you feel most alone. Keep a diary of those times so that you can identify them. That's the very time of day when you should find a special place to be. This would be a good time to go out and do some volunteer work. We hear all the time of cutbacks taking place in employment situations. In many agencies, staff will be moving out because of economic reasons. But those agencies could still survive if people like you would go in and volunteer their time and talent.

Some people feel they don't have any talent. We all have talent. Maybe you haven't discovered yours yet, and that, too, could be a reason for your loneliness. The only way to discover your talent is to make some step toward seeking it. Being of service does wonders toward removing the attitude of loneliness. And until you begin to change this attitude, you can't draw to you those who might erase the sense of loneliness.

LEARN TO BE OTHER-CENTERED

People often don't realize that they give off an air of what they are. Some call these vibrations. When you are giving off a negative air, others pick it up and don't want to be around you because you are so self-concerned. Self-concern can be turned into a beautiful experience. It can lead you to wonderful discoveries about yourself. But don't take it so far that it gives others the idea that you "don't want to be bothered."

LIVING ALONE DOESN'T HAVE TO MEAN BEING ALONE

Another thing I want to suggest is that you work with your past beliefs and negative attitudes about what it means to live by yourself. Whenever you find yourself complaining about being by yourself, that's the time to remember some of the beautiful Scriptural references that can give you comfort, peace, a desire to do something about yourself or for someone else. The secret to overcoming loneliness is to associate yourself with something more comprehensive, to come in tune with that Spirit, that presence that is within you waiting to be tapped.

Remember my comment about the people who live for Friday? Well, at the other end of the spectrum are those who hate to see Friday come around because it signals being alone. I find this often with young women who live alone. When these women leave their jobs on Friday, everybody in the office seems to have plans for the weekend. These women may not have a thing in mind, but rather than admit this to their co-workers, they'll say they've got big weekends ahead. When they get back to the office Monday morning, they feel they have to say they've participated in certain activities because everyone else is talking about exciting weekends.

If you have no plans for the weekend, why does that have to be so terrible? It's all right. That may be your time to unfold your Christ self, to really find out what is going on inside of you and to get to know the beautiful Spirit inside you. Jesus said the first of all the commandments is *"Thou shalt love the Lord thy God with all thy heart, and with all thy soul, and with all thy mind, and with all thy strength"* (Mark 12:30); and the second is *"Thou shalt love thy neighbor as thyself"* (Mark 12:31). The first neighbor you have is the person inside you.

You have to look at where you are in your frame of reference with God as Spirit. In 1 John 4:4 we read, *"Greater is He that is in you, than he that is in the world."* "He" represents Spirit. So first of all, there is that about you which is so beautiful that it alone should tell you that you have no cause for loneliness. You have the Spirit of the living God abiding right within you. But the only way you're going to know it's there is to speak those words, to dwell on beautiful thoughts, and to really give yourself an opportunity to listen to the still, small voice within you, which is also a comforting voice.

The apostle Paul said that he had learned how to be content in whatever location he found himself. He learned how to be humble and how to abound. Likewise, it doesn't matter where you live—in a home with family, alone in an apartment, or a senior citizens' high-rise. If you will begin to touch your inner resource, you'll begin to find out that you really are not alone. Once you tap that inner resource, everything in the outer falls in place. You begin to have the order you need, the joy that you want.

LOOK TO YOURSELF FIRST

You can't go outside to cure loneliness. You have to go inside. And you have to recognize that there is a presence and a power within you. I have been alone physically and mentally many times in my life. But never alone spiritually. Whenever I feel depressed, I've always come back to something inspirational—a Scripture, a particular place I enjoy being, a book, a song, or listening to recordings of inspirational music. Once you put yourself in an inspirational frame of mind, your thoughts begin to move through the spiritual current, and a peace comes over you. Peace erases loneliness. Love erases loneliness. When you learn that you can love and appreciate yourself, you don't have time to be lonely.

And as Jesus said in John 14:15–18:

If ye love me, keep my commandments. And I will pray the Father, and He shall give you another Comforter, that he may abide with you forever . . . ye know him; for he dwelleth with you, and shall be in you.

Finally, let me caution that it will take time for you to overcome your loneliness-thinking pattern— but it *can* be overcome. Turn to the fourteenth chapter of John and read those comforting words. Know that you are unrepeatable, that you are a miracle, that you are a unique child of God, and that God in you makes the difference. Be reminded of the goodness of the Father in you, and know that you are not alone.

Regardless of whether or not there are any people around you, you can know that God loves you and that God has not left you alone. That presence and that power of Spirit in you is God. It will comfort you so that you will not have to have anybody around. As you accept that truth, you will eventually have with you beautiful people.

CHAPTER NINE

What Is This Thing Called Death?

I don't often go back and look at notes of sermons that I used to write in great detail, but I did go through my files one day and discovered that it had been many years since I had spoken from the pulpit on the subject of death. It was during a time when some heavy emotions were being felt in the city of Atlanta. This sadness, this grief, this mourning was caused by a series of brutal, puzzling murders. Death is difficult enough for most poeple to accept under any circumstances; murder makes it all the harder to accept.

Yet it is our basic, underlying attitude toward death that causes the greatest difficulty. That attitude must be changed if we are to accept death for what it is, for as Jesus said, *"Neither is new wine put into old wineskins; if it is, the skins burst, and the*

*wine is spilled, and the skins are destroyed; but new
wine is put into fresh wineskins, and so both are pre-
served* (Matthew 9:17, RSV). These words suggest
that one reason we don't progress spiritually is that
we're still holding on to old conflicts and old beliefs
that bind and that place limitations on us and keep
us from enjoying the fullness of life which God is,
which God has promised. This fullness of life is what
Paul referred to when he said, *"For in Him we live,
and move, and have our being"* (Acts 17:28).

But when you listen and begin to believe in God's
truth, then the old beliefs have to go. Two ideas cannot occupy the same mind at one time. So a new understanding of death will cause the old fear of death
to move out of your consciousness. This concept of
death being something we have to fear is a human
thought. It is not God's plan, for life is eternal. Jesus made this very plain when he said, *"I am come
that they might have life, and that they might have
it more abundantly"* (John 10:10). He didn't say,
"that they might have a little piece of life." He said
abundantly. If you and I are not having life abundantly, it is because we are not living by the spiritual
law.

For example, as children many of us ended our

day by praying, "Now I lay me down to sleep; I pray the Lord my soul to keep. If I should die before I wake, I pray the Lord my soul to take." And we believed in that prayer and went on to sleep. We didn't worry about waking up, because we knew that we were going to get up and go back to our toys, our games, our friends, and our familiar surroundings.

Think about that. As children, we believed in abundant life. This is what Jesus meant when he said we have to become as little children. The mind of a child is so much more teachable than that of an adult. As children, we prayed that prayer with power. So why, as adults, do we fear death?

Some of us don't even say the word. Say it: *death.* Say it aloud: *death.* There are so many folks walking around worrying about dying that they're not living. Most of us are dead on our feet because we don't realize that life is consciousness. Such people are living only in the physical. But there is that divineness of us, there is that Spirit of us which cannot die. Since that's the case, what's so wrong with shedding the physical body when we know we're going on to something greater? New wine is put into *fresh* wineskins!

LIFE, THE CENTER OF OUR BEING

Let's turn to the intellect for a moment, for that too is part of our God-given self. From an intellectual perspective, death can be viewed metaphysically. Metaphysics is simply a systematic study of the science of Being—that which transcends or goes beyond the physical. Now, one who practices metaphysics, one skilled in the science of Being, is a metaphysician, a student and teacher of the laws of Spirit. In the New Thought movement, we're all metaphysicians, because we go beyond the physical to enable us to get away from the human limitations and embrace our spiritual selves. By working at the spiritual level, we behold the Spirit of God in man, God incarnate in man as life, as love, as wisdom, as truth, as abundance, as prosperity—all the attributes of God flowing through our spiritual selves.

To illustrate this, suppose we draw a circle to represent the spiritual self. Then, around that circle, let's draw another circle, so that our illustration looks like this:

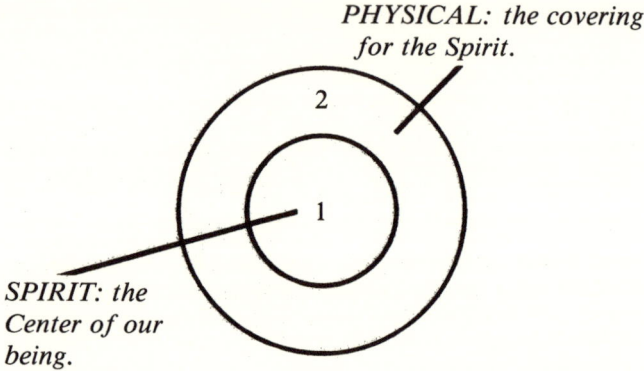

PHYSICAL: *the covering for the Spirit.*

SPIRIT: *the Center of our being.*

The inner circle, numbered 1, is that part of us which is like our Creator, for, as we know, we are made in the image and likeness of God; and that image is a spiritual image. Circle number 2, the outer circle, is the environment in which we exist. This environment is made up of many things, including where we live, how we live, what influences us, and so forth. This outer circle, in fact, is what we usually refer to when we say "life," for this is our conscious experience.

So there is an inner self of us and an outer self. Recognizing this is the key to everything we do, the key to life and death. That inner self, to use Paul's words again, is where we live, move, and have our being. But that outer circle surrounds the inner and acts as an inhibitor that keeps us from letting God work through us. Here in this outer circle are our hang-ups, our mistakes, our false beliefs, our friends, and all things physical and material. Many of us spend all our conscious time and energy in that outer circle. Even in the face of death we are in that outer circle, worrying about who's going to get the car, who's going to be wearing my clothes, how will the folks survive without me, will my wife/husband remarry?

But I want to tell you that living constantly in the outer circle creates a fear of death. How? Because we spend so much time worrying about the outer, about our material possessions, about our human relationships, that we can't enjoy them, because we know that sooner or later death will take us away from them. Fortunately, most of us eventually reach a point in life where we begin to place less emphasis on the outer and more on the inner. At that point, we begin to seek answers to many concerns, including our fear of death.

What we find, though, is that we can't explain everything. Even God is incomprehensible to us. We really don't fully understand God; we're just picking at what we think we know to be true. No one can really explain it all. But one thing we *do* come to understand as we begin to seek God's truth is that immortality is a characteristic of God. And since we all have within us that inner circle, that spiritual image of God, then it follows that immortality must also be a characteristic of each of us. With this understanding comes yet another understanding: *when the soul goes through the transition we call death, it is not dying, but simply giving up a physical expression to move on to an even greater, more glorious expression.*

DEALING WITH A LOVED ONE'S DEATH

I believe that our loved ones who have passed on are as close to us as we think them to be, for again, life is consciousness. If a loved one has gone out of the physical body, you will find that when you draw into your consciousness thoughts about that loved one, then nothing is between the two of you except a sort of transparent barrier that can be overcome by thought. There are numerous instances of research by doctors and scientists on life after death. People have told of "dying" on the operating table, for instance, and journeying through what they describe as dark tunnels to light. One lady said, "I didn't see a figure of God. What I saw and felt was so much love that I had to make up in my mind that I wanted to come back and be with my children. And I got myself together and came on back."

Elizabeth Kübler-Ross, one of the foremost authorities on the question of life after death, has worked with a number of cancer patients and, through her research, has helped millions make the transition into their next cycle. She says that death is simply the shedding of the physical body, like a butterfly coming out of a cocoon. It is a transition into a higher state of consciousness, in which you continue to perceive and to understand and to be able to grow. The only thing you lose is something you don't need anymore, your physical body. It's like putting away your winter coat when spring comes.

So there is no separation except in your human thought. And many times when someone leaves a physical body, we go through the sadness and the mourning because we don't want to release the person. Our human feelings take over. But in our spiritual mind, we know that the life of that person is still expressing with the Father in its own way. Once we become aware of this truth, the grief, the mourning, and the daily sense of loss will move away from us.

Another thing we have to realize is that sometimes our loved ones *want* to release the physical body. Perhaps they are only continuing in this existence because they know that we are not ready for them to go, and so they hang on in order to give us time to make the adjustment. But such a person will find a way to release the body, whether through illness, accident, or by act of his own hand. That's another reason that it does us little good to indulge in excessive grief—we don't know what's on our loved ones' consciousness before they leave here.

So many times when I deliver a eulogy—I call them words of life—I say to families, "That is not your loved one in that casket. That's just a body. Your loved one has released the physical, but at a spiritual level, he still exists." What I'm saying is that God receives his own back to Him. Life doesn't end; it continues. Life goes back to life. There's no breaking the cycle of life. What we have to break is our old habit of thinking about death as something dreadful.

And when a loved one moves into another cycle of life, more than ever do we need to remember that our Father, a God of love, so takes care of His creation that as we move to the next experience, that same God of love is right there. What the survivors have to do is to hold fast to the truth of Jesus' teachings about resurrection, about life being eternal, about life being abundant. And the survivors owe it to themselves to continue to take every day as a day of joy and to turn their thoughts to living, as God intended them to do.

WHAT'S IT LIKE ON THE "OTHER SIDE"?

Now, I'm not going to argue with anybody about the streets of gold. If that's your belief about what you'll encounter on the "other side," that's all right. We're all at different levels of consciousness. Didn't Jesus say, *"In my Father's house are many mansions"*? I only know that in this physical body there's that which takes place in me which is so wonderful and so peaceful and just downright exciting that I *know* I have nothing to fear when I move on to my next experience.

A lady sitting next to me on an airplane said to me, after we'd been talking for a while, "Boy, I wonder what *you're* going to be a little later on." I said, "Honey, I don't know; but whatever it is, it's bound to be good!" You see, I *feel* good about myself. I'm so excited about using the truths of God and seeing the results that I just keep saying, "Well, Father, what's next?" Whether it's here or there, it doesn't matter. Just the idea of expression, of living and enjoying life is enough. Feeling this kind of joy on this conscious, physical level, I begin to comprehend what the apostle meant when he said, *"It doth not yet appear what we shall be; but we know that, when He shall appear, we shall be like Him; for we shall see Him as He is"* (1 John 3:2).

So what we need to realize is that *all* experience, including that we call death, is part of eternity. And eternity is right now. You've got all the eternity that you're ever going to have, right here, right now. The past and the future come together in the now. And death is no more than a graduation from one level of experience to another.

Work with yourself to know this truth, and fear of death cannot stay in your mind. It's your attitude about it that makes it fearful, because death itself is just a transition. Spirit cannot die. Yes, eventually we all face the experience of physical death. But even then, God gives us the strength to grow, to look beyond the moment and know that there is something more—abundantly more—for us to experience.

With spiritual maturity, our prayer can progress from the "Now I lay me down to sleep" of childhood to a twenty-four-hour-a-day awareness that God is always the keeper of our soul. As James Dillet Freeman so beautifully expresses it in his "Prayer for Protection":

> The light of God surrounds me;
> The love of God enfolds me;
> The power of God protects me;
> The presence of God watches over me.
> Wherever I am, God is.

CHAPTER TEN

What Are You
Afraid Of?

Webster says that fear is "a very painful emotion, usually followed by alarm." Fear, then, simply means that we have allowed some object or some other person or some situation to become so large in our consciousness in the way we see it, in the appearance of it, that we become fearful of it and lose control of ourselves. Then the fear, the thing we dread, seems to be in total command of us. But we don't *have* to be afraid. Fear is an emotion, and emotions are ours to control; the emotion does not control us—we are in charge of the emotion.

I have discovered that the best way to work with fear is to get a better understanding of God, a better understanding of who we are in relationship to God. Let me cite a few instances.

Just recently I was watching one of the morning talk shows on which a psychiatrist was discussing fear and how it tightens and grips so many people to the point where they have to go in for therapeutic treatment. On this program was a very beautiful young housewife in her early twenties who lived in fear of going anyplace by herself. From the time her husband left for work in the morning, she would not leave her house alone until he returned. Even if they went out to dinner, for some reason she had a phobia of people around them. She was constantly fearful that someone was in the garage or waiting in their home. This fear had such control of her that she had to seek professional help for it.

WE CREATE FEAR WHERE THERE WAS NONE BEFORE

Most of us aren't so caught up in our fears as was this young housewife. We realize that we can control our fears by looking at them for the nothingness they are and then banish them by speaking the truth about them. The so-called threat we are afraid of, in other words, has no power except the power we give it.

But sometimes we are made fearful by the suggestion that we *should* be afraid. For instance, I read of a man who owned a German Shepherd that he had trained to be very fierce and to protect him and his family. When this man was transferred to another city, he gave the dog to a friend of his. A year later he returned and decided to visit his friend. When he reached the friend's house, there was a high fence around the yard and a sign reading "Beware of Dog." On the porch was a dog. Confidently, the man ignored the sign and stepped inside the gate. As he did so, the dog jumped up, roaring and growling, with his hair on end and his teeth bared.

The man said to him, "Now listen, Prince. You know who I am. I'm your first master. I'm the one who brought you here. And I'm *so* happy to see you again!" He kept talking with these beautiful, soothing words of love; and the dog kept growling and rearing up. The man came closer, talking all the while, until finally the dog relaxed and his tail started wagging. At this point, the man approached the dog, petted him, and rang the doorbell.

After the friends had greeted each other warmly, the dog's owner asked in amazement, "But how did you get in the yard?"

"I walked right by Prince," the visitor answered. "I told him who I was, and I came right in."

Even more amazed, his friend said, "You told him who you were?"

"Why, yes," the visitor said. "I talked to him and came right to the door."

"But that's not Prince!" the friend said. "Prince died shortly after you gave him to us. We were grieved about it because of our friendship with you, so we immediately purchased another dog who looked just like him. *That* dog, the one you just introduced yourself to, is a killer. We have raised him to protect us. That's why the high fence and the warning sign."

Well, as you can imagine, the visitor was overwhelmed at the thought of what he had just done with this strange dog. He continued his visit, deciding that since he'd gotten past the dog the first time, he could go right back the way he came. But something had happened. As he considered what his friend had said about this dog not being the familiar Prince, it dawned on him that he was afraid. And when he went out and walked past the dog, the dog growled and came to his feet. Rather than responding as confidently as he had done the first time, the man started running; and the dog, of course, chased him. He barely made it to the gate.

Isn't this the story of many of us? We are sometimes at peace about a given situation, when suddenly some change in the situation makes us look at
it differently. Then our imagination begins to form
pictures of what *could* happen, what *might* happen,
what we *expect* to happen (usually the worst).
Regardless what our experiences have been up to
that point, we let our emotions get involved, and the
fear becomes so great in us that we can't see anything else except the object of our fear.

Fear Is Man-Made, Not God-Given

What we need to become convinced of is the words
in 2 Timothy, first chapter, verse seven: *"God hath
not given us the spirit of fear; but of power."* I take
this to mean that we cannot overcome fear with human power, but by the Spirit of the living God that
is within us. That's what most of us don't realize.
When we call forth the power of this living Christ
within us, we don't have to be fearful.

Here's another example, again involving a dog,
to illustrate what I mean. My household includes
a French poodle named Ralph. He's extremely
friendly and has grown to love all the people who

come into the house. One day a mother and her four-year-old daughter came to visit. At the sight of Ralph, the little girl jumped on the couch and screamed in terror. After she had been calmed, I said to the mother, "Are you working with your daughter about her fear of dogs?"

The mother said, "Well, she was bitten by a dog when she was much younger. Now she's scared to death of dogs, and that's that."

"Ah, but it's not that simple!" I answered. "That fear will grow and grow in her conscious thinking until it takes over. Suppose something of utmost importance to her comes up, but it involves passing a dog or being in the presence of one? If you don't begin now to help her work with her fear, she may not be able to rise above it at a crucial moment. And fear, like any emotion, is contagious. If you allow her to continue living with this one fear, to get used to the presence of fear in her mind, it could easily spread to other areas of her life."

And the same holds true for adults. Many of our fears were learned in childhood. We learned to fear the darkness; certain types of disease; poverty; some of us even were taught to fear people who were different from us. Some people never outgrow such fears, which turn into phobias and prejudices and areas of ignorance. But with the right guidance and an awareness of our inner resources, we can *un*learn our fears.

Think of Daniel, who was thrown into the lion's den because he would not bow down and worship the king and the idols of his day. Daniel believed in a living God; he kept in constant communion with his God, taking time, three times a day, to pray. So knowing what kind of God he served, he faced the lions with faith. He knew that the God to Whom he prayed was a living presence within him, and that It was the *same* Spirit that created the lions.

The next morning the king, who dearly loved Daniel but was simply following the rules of his kingdom when he had Daniel thrown to the lions, went to the den and called Daniel's name. Daniel answered him, saying that God had sent his angels and shut the mouths of the lions. He even praised the king, whom he had served faithfully before His enemies had set the trap that caused him to be thrown to the lions. With the forgiving love and the overcoming power of God in his heart, Daniel said, *"O king, live forever"* (Daniel 6:21). He had triumphed over a very present and deadly threat.

WE CAN DO WHAT DANIEL DID

As I explained in the introduction to this book, all of us have lions in our lives—things that overcome and overwhelm us. But when these lions come upon you, take time to pray, to say *There is only one power and one presence in my life, God the Good omnipotent.* Know that if there seems to be any other power, any other presence, if there is something that is frightening you, it's because you are giving it the power of your belief, just like our friend who suddenly feared a dog he had so recently petted.

Rather than letting this fear belief control you, speak the word of truth about it. If you have to speak out loud to convince yourself with the fullness of your voice, then do so. If you have to sit quietly and pray about it, do so. Use the power that God has given you. He created you after His image and gave you power over everything. Know that the thing that seems to be frightening has no power, no control over you. Know the truth of your being—that God *is* the only presence; God *is* the only power.

CHAPTER ELEVEN

Where Do I Go
from Here?

A few months ago, I went to speak at a prestig-
ious church in a major city. The minister took
me out to dinner the evening before and impressed
upon me that I was speaking to a very important
congregation, that his people were very wealthy and
highly intellectual. He wanted me to know what I
would be facing the next morning when I stood in
his pulpit. You see, at this particular church, no person of color had ever stood in the pulpit. In fact,
there were no persons of color in this particular congregation. And there I was, a person of color, and
what's more, a woman minister!

Well, I looked at him, I listened to him. He
asked me if I had any comments. I said, "No, I have
no comment to make because I know that the Spirit
of the Lord will give me a message." He said that
the church bulletin was being run off that night and

that he would like to know the title of my message so that he could include it. I said, "I can't tell you, because nothing is coming through to me at this time. So will you permit me to just be myself and just let Spirit work through me when I come in the morning?" He agreed to this.

When I arrived the next morning and took my seat by the pulpit, I looked out at the congregation. Sure enough, everybody was looking directly at me; and my first thought was "Wow! Father, are You sure I'm in the right place? Maybe I don't measure up after all." And then the second thought came: *Be still and know that I am God.*

When the time came for me to speak, I stood silently for a moment. Then I said, "You know, there are so many of us who have reached what we call the pinnacle of success. We're in the right church; we're sitting in the right pew; we have the right friends; we've earned our degrees; we have the right job, the right salary; we're generally in the right position in life."

Then I said, "But do you know what I'm finding out in my travels and in my work? That for many of us who have reached the so-called pinnacle of success, there still appears to be something missing from our lives."

This brings me to the question I want to raise in this concluding chapter. Once you have it all, where do you go from there? In Mark, the tenth chapter, verses seventeen to twenty-five, there is an incident between Jesus and a rich young ruler that illustrates what I'm saying.

> And when he was gone forth into the way, there came one running, and kneeled to him, and asked him, Good Master, what shall I do that I may inherit eternal life?
>
> And Jesus said unto him, Why callest thou me good? There is none good but one, that is, God.
>
> Thou knowest the commandments, Do not commit adultery, Do not kill, Do not steal, Do not bear false witness, Defraud not, Honor thy father and mother.
>
> And he answered and said unto him, Master, all these have I observed from my youth.
>
> Then Jesus beholding him loved him, and said unto him, One thing thou lackest: go thy way, sell whatsoever thou hast, and give to the poor, and thou shalt have treasure in heaven; and come, take up the cross, and follow me.
>
> And he was sad at that saying, and went away grieved; for he had great possessions.
>
> And Jesus looked round about, and saith unto

His disciples, How hardly shall they that have riches enter into the kingdom of God!

And the disciples were astonished at His words. But Jesus answereth again, and saith unto them, Children, how hard it is for them that trust in riches to enter into the kingdom of God!

It is easier for a camel to go through the eye of a needle, than for a rich man to enter into the kingdom of God.

WHERE IS YOUR TRUST?

Now, we don't see in this conversation where Jesus made any statement that it's a sin to be rich. That's not the essence of the conversation. Our Father is rich, and we are the heirs of a rich universe. Furthermore, God is no respecter of person, by which I mean that it doesn't matter *who* we are or what we have—we are all equal in His sight. So all of us have the opportunity to draw upon the abundance of God, which is everywhere equally present.

But in talking about the young man, Jesus used a key word: *trust*—specifically, in this case, trust in riches, in the material. There are so many of us who are pushing, who are moving, who are striving totally to satisfy our needs through material possessions. What's happening in many such cases is that the inner self, the spiritual part of us, is not at peace. That is the implication of this message. Jesus said to the young man, all right, you've kept the commandments, you have everything that anybody could desire; but there's something else beyond keeping the commandments. And that is knowing within yourself that if the material is lost to you, you still have the Spirit of the living God.

Whatever moves away from you or out of your life, as Jesus explained to His disciples, can be multiplied a hundredfold by the Lord, because God works through each of us. And if we are willing to put God first in all our material quests, then we don't have anything to worry about. The young man just couldn't see that. He really wanted to experience God, he really wanted to know what it was to have that full salvation. But he could not give up the material.

STRIVE FOR BALANCE

Psychologists and scientists have long spoken of left-brained and right-brained people. Those who are dominated by the left side of their brains are the intellectuals; they are the ones who are very much concerned about analysis, about criticism, about looking at things thoroughly, seeing to the very point of a thing's inception. Then there are the predominantly right-brained individuals who are more into the intuitive, who are aesthetes, who are the artists, and who look for beauty.

There is nothing wrong with being either left-brained or right-brained; but we need to strive for a balance between the two, a good combination of both. Clearly, the young man in the parable was caught up with his left-brain. His position in life spoke of the intellect, of thinking, of planning, of knowing how to manage his resources to achieve great wealth. But his right brain, his intuitiveness, his desire for the Spirit was also coming up, and he didn't know how to balance the two. So rather than make that step to balance himself, he chose to leave Jesus and say, I don't think I can accept what you're telling me.

How many of us have reached that point? In so many ways we might feel that we have it all, that we don't need anything or anybody, that we "have arrived." And yet, deep within, most of us who are making those kinds of assertions are also hurting;

we're in pain, confused, anxious, worried. Why? Because we will not allow the intuitiveness, the God-self of us to come through. Jesus said, if you love me, keep my commandments. He said on another occasion, *"Seek ye first the kingdom of God and His righteousness, and all these things shall be added unto you."*

When Solomon became king, he prayed for God to give him the wisdom, the understanding to know how to govern his people. That's why I say to you that the important thing for you to remember is that your first priority must be to abide in that Presence. What really excites me about being a child of God is that God is not way off someplace, that His Spirit is everywhere evenly present. His Spirit abides in me. And if you truly want to know where you go from here—wherever "here" may be for you—then you will begin by turning within to that ever-abiding Presence.

And, you know, the Scriptures also tell us, *"Greater is He that is in you than he that is in the world,"* meaning, in his case, that it's only through the goodness of God that you have achieved whatever you have anyway. So if you will practice every day making that union, making that connection, making that oneness with the presence and power of God that is within you, you'll never again have to raise the question, "Where do I go from here?" You'll get into a trusting attitude and you'll just know that all you have to do is take one day at a time and God will direct your steps. The Scriptures say, trust in Him. Don't depend solely on your human understanding; don't get caught up in the assurance of having a degree. I have mine too, but that degree doesn't mean a hill of beans unless I know the source, the Intelligence that I used to earn it.

That's why we have to be very careful in our pursuit of wealth. We get so tied to it, so involved in it that we forget the source. The young man in the parable had truly forgotten the source of his wealth. Jesus spoke to him so beautifully. And those same words are being spoken to you and to me today. Trust in God. Let me go back to that verse, because that's the key: *"Children, how hard it is for them that trust in riches to enter into the kingdom of God."* Trust in God first.

When you wake up, begin the day by saying, "Father-Mother God, it's Your day. You've given it to me to use. Let me begin my day with You." Perhaps you won't get a direct response right away;

sometimes you just get a sense of peace, a knowingness that all is well. And then as you go to work and face decisions, quickly go within and ask God for guidance. On days when my desk is piled with work, I pause a few moments before I touch anything, and I say, "Father, show me where to start." And a thought will come through. I'll look at the pile and I'll know exactly where to begin. And this is true not just of the work I do at my desk, but of whatever I do, wherever I'm going. I always take that time to say, "Father, show me."

This method will work for you too. When you pray, just say in the simplest way, "Lord, I love You so much. I love Your presence, Your power in me." Then you will know that everything you do will be in Divine order, because the Spirit of the living God is moving through you, speaking through you, guiding you in all things.

This is the basis of our being children of God. We simply have to go back to our Father and ask for direction. So when you ask yourself, "Where do I go from here?" stop and recognize that you haven't accomplished it all. You're going from glory to glory. You're moving step by step toward your perfection. You haven't reached it yet; true perfection is to trust totally in Spirit; true perfection is to be balanced, to use the intellect but to allow it to be spiritualized by the presence of the living God.

To help you on your journey, take this affirmation with you:

> *I abide in the Father, and all my activity is spiritually motivated. I know what to do, how to do it, and when to do it. Whatever I begin with God will turn out all right.*

CHAPTER TWELVE

Affirmations
and How to Use Them

An affirmation is a positive statement of truth. To affirm is to make firm in your mind. It is stating it to be true regardless of all evidence to the contrary. It is a type of mind activity used for building consciousness (awareness). It lifts you out of false thinking. An affirmation contains the elements of your belief, attitude, and motivation. An affirmation is made up of words. Words charged with power, conviction, and faith will produce after their kind. Every time you speak, the atoms in your body are affected; the rate of vibration is either raised or lowered.

God has given us the power of the word to use. We should be selective in the choice of words we use, for they will become our experience.

The purpose of an affirmation is to impress the subconscious mind, for what is impressed is expressed. This is done by repetition, feeling, and imaging. Repeat over and over as often as possible the affirmation with conviction and authority, believing every word you say, and see it taking shape and form. Repeat it until it becomes a part of you. In conclusion always give thanks.

"Thou shalt also decree a thing, and it shall be established unto thee: and the Light shall shine upon thy ways." (Job 22:28)

"Now faith is the substance of things HOPED for, the evidence of things not SEEN." (Hebrews 11:1)

TROUBLED YOUTH

*I Refuse to Allow My Peers to Influence Me
in Doing Anything That Is Not Right for Me*

Dear God, grant me the strength and the courage to say NO to the things which are unlike You. Grant me the ability to stand up for the right principles regardless of what others may think and say. I do not have to agree with or patronize others to gain popularity. It is not important to be popular. It is important to follow the dictates of Spirit within me—LOVE and WISDOM.

I am not inferior to anyone, for I know I have the same mind which was also in Christ Jesus. I will not abuse my body by taking substances that do not agree with it. I forgive those who may have hurt or harmed me in any way. I love them and release them to their highest good. If I have accepted resentment or hurt from anyone, I forgive and love myself for who I am—a beautiful child of God. I have a high esteem of myself. I have a relationship with my creator, God, for He is in charge of my life.

THANK YOU, GOD, FOR THE ABILITY TO SAY NO WHEN I NEED TO SAY NO. AND SO IT IS!

> *"For thy name's sake lead me,*
> *and guide me." Psalm 31:3*

PARENTS OF TROUBLED YOUTH

Today, I Make a Conscious Decision
to Lay My Burden Down

Almighty Father with whom nothing is impossible, I surrender *(name)* and this thing called drug addiction over to You. I of myself can do nothing, but You are all the power there is, You are within him and within me, let him respond to the Divinity which indwells him. Let there be light. Let there be understanding. Heal him from the desire to use drugs. He now has no longing to express anything that destroys his body and confuses his mind. He is now free from dissatisfaction and unhappiness. He seeks to express his true nature—the Christ in him. He has the self-esteem he needs, for he is a child of God.

Almighty Father, I now surrender myself to You. I ask for strength, patience, love, peace of mind, and divine right action in my mind, my body, and all my affairs. I do not know what to do, Lord, but You are all-wise, so think, speak, and act through me all the way. God, You promised, "Before they call, I will answer; and while they are yet speaking, I will hear" (Isa. 65:24). You also promised, "He shall call upon me, and I will answer him: I will be with him in trouble; I will deliver him, and honour him" (Psalm 91:15). Jesus said, "If ye abide in me, and my words abide in you, ye shall ask what ye will, and it shall be done unto you" (John 15:7).

Lord, I believe, I know You never fail. I give thanks with all my heart and soul for answered prayer. And So It Is!

"Is anything too hard for the Lord?" Genesis 18:14

ALCOHOL ADDICTION

*God within Me Now Sets Me Free
from the Habit of Taking Alcohol*

I am conscious of my oneness, my whole being with Spirit. I do not have to look to anything outside myself for pleasure and satisfaction. There is no sense of insecurity, inferiority, or depression. I am not afraid of anything. I do not have to prove anything to anyone. All fear and doubts are now removed to the nothingness from whence they came. The joy of the Lord is my strength. I have faith in God in me to break this habit. I now command this habit, the desire for alcohol, to be banished from my consciousness.

I am now free from the habit of intemperance, for I now place my attention on Infinite Intelligence, Spirit, within me to satisfy my every need and desire. My body is the temple of the Living God, and God is in control. Thank You, Father, for answered prayer. And So It Is!

*"With men this is impossible; but with God
all things are possible." Matt. 19:26*

DRUG ADDICTION

*I Now Make a Conscious Decision to Release
the Use of All Drugs That Are Destroying
My Body, in the Name and through the Power
of Jesus Christ*

I now recognize that being dependent on drugs is not
the answer to my problems. I cannot escape from the
anxieties and fears that confront me, nor the issues
of life, by the use of drugs. Happiness is not derived
through a needle I place in my veins or something
I put in my mouth or sniff through my nostrils.
There is nothing on the outside that can change my
insecurity or my low self-esteem.

I know that within me is a Living, Loving, Infinite Presence waiting to respond to me. Within me
is all the strength, the courage, the love, the wisdom
I need to overcome any condition. I love myself. I
love my body, for it is the temple of the Living God.
I now make a conscious decision to release the desire
and habit of using drugs, in the Name and through
the Mighty Power of Jesus Christ. Thanks, God.

*"For thou, O Lord, art good and forgiving,
abounding in steadfast love to all who
call on thee." Psalm 86:5 (RSV)*

GETTING THE RIGHT WIFE

The Spirit of the Lord Goes before Me to
Make Happy and Successful My Way

There is a woman in the universe who was created to be my wife and I was created to be her husband. We cannot miss each other for we were created to be together. Divine Love, that which attracts, combines, and draws together, is at work in our lives now. I represent the type of man she is looking for, and she represents the type of woman I am looking for. There is compatibility, there is freedom and trust.

The activity of Divine Love in me now manifests my true wife. We enjoy marriage together. And So It Is! Thank You, Father.

"Prayer . . . has great power in its effects."
James 5:16 (RSV)

GETTING THE RIGHT HUSBAND

I Believe There Is a Man in the Universe
Waiting to Love and Marry Me

Jesus said, "Ask, and it shall be given you" (Matt. 7:7). "If ye shall ask anything in my name I will do it" (John 14:14). ". . . ye have not, because ye ask not . . ." (James 4:2).

Today I place an order in the universe for my true husband. I know I can contribute to his happiness, and he contributes to my happiness. He loves my ideals and I love his ideals. He does not want to make me over and I do not want to make him over. We enjoy mutal love, freedom, and respect. I behold the Christ in him, and he beholds the Christ in me. Creative Intelligence now brings us together. There is mutual attraction. We cannot miss each other. Those who belong together will stay together. Thanks, God. And So It Is!

> *"Ask, and ye shall receive, that your joy*
> *may be full." John 16:24*

SEXUAL APPETITE

*I Now Lift Up the Serpent in the Wilderness,
the Son of Man to Become the Son of God*

It is important to observe our thoughts, our impulses, and our desires, for whatever we dwell on, we create. Thought dominates our lives, and we are responsible for the results.

Sex is an ecstasy experienced when participated in by two persons who love each other. When man and woman (Wisdom and Love) have a soul communion, a mystical marriage, sex is a spiritual experience. Sex should not be indulged in for the outer pleasure, to satisfy feelings. This lowers the experience to animalism, fleshly sex. "Then when lust hath conceived, it bringeth forth sin: and sin, when it is finished, bringeth forth death" (James 1:15). Promiscuity, dissipation, animal sex, is the father of death. It depletes the body of its vitality.

God, grant me the ability to think on the things of virtue, of love, things that are spiritual, and so transmute this appetite of sex to Your glory. Thanks, God.

*"That which is born of the flesh is flesh; and that
which is born of the Spirit is spirit." John 3:6*

AIDS

*Almighty, Infinite, Divine Spirit within Me
Is Healing Me Now*

There is no incurable disease. Erroneous thoughts produce disease. Positive thoughts move and build the body. Whenever I speak, I cause the atoms in my body to change places, as well as lower or raise the vibrations that affect my body.

I now release from my mind all unforgiving thoughts. I forgive myself for all the mistakes I have made. I forgive others who seemed to have hurt me in any way. To forgive is to love. I now call on Divine Love to manifest itself in me.

I love myself and give others the freedom to be. I admit that, of myself, I am powerless to solve my problem.

The Almighty, Infinite, Divine Spirit within me is now pulsating, restoring, renewing, and revitalizing my immune system, every organ, cell, tissue and atom of my being. My bloodstream is cleansed. I feel this, I believe it, I accept it and give thanks for it. It is done unto me as I believe. Lord, I believe. And So It Is!

The Twelve Spiritual Powers

Jesus had 12 disciples. These were not men who chose Jesus—rather, each was carefully chosen by Jesus. This is important because it shows that Jesus had a special purpose in choosing these particular twelve men. Unity believes that Jesus' careful selection has to do with the fact that each disciple metaphysically symbolizes one of the twelve Powers of Mind through which the Christ in man expresses.

Charles Fillmore, co-founder of Unity, went further to claim that each disciple-faculty also has a specific center in the physical body, over which it rules.

The disciples, the faculty of mind each represents, the location in the body, and the color that coordinates with that particular faculty are listed below:

DISCIPLE	FACULTY	LOCATION IN BODY	COLOR
Peter	FAITH	Pineal gland	Deep blue
Andrew	STRENGTH	Small of back	Forest green
James	WISDOM	Solar plexus	Yellow
John	LOVE	Back of heart	Pink
Philip	POWER	Root of tongue	Purple
Bartholomew	IMAGINATION	Between the eyes	Light blue
Thomas	UNDERSTANDING	Forehead	Gold
Matthew	WILL	Forehead	Silver
James the less	ORDER	Navel	Light green
Simon the Zealot	ZEAL	Medulla, back of head	Orange
Thaddaeus	RENUNCIATION	Lower spine	Russet
Judas	LIFE	Generative center	Red

About the Author

by

Marion Delaney-Harris
Consultant to Dr. King

The Reverend Dr. Barbara Lewis King has been called one of the most influential spiritual leaders in the world. At the age of 13 she knew she wanted to be a minister, and her carefully guided paths eventually led her there.

Overcoming a life-threatening physical condition as a teenager, Barbara was inspired to live by increasing her faith in God in her to heal any condition. This faith, this prayer, this vi-

125

sion became the cornerstone by which Barbara was able to build her life's work. She holds a bachelor's degree in sociology, a master's degree and certification in social work, two honorary doctorates in divinity and a number of years of training in religion and the ministry. She is currently pursuing a doctorate in educational administration.

Barbara has been an educational administrator, a college teacher, director of the largest merger of three settlement houses in Chicago, and a college dean. She proudly notes that all of these prepared her for the ministry.

A native of Houston, a former resident of Chicago, and now of Atlanta—all claim her as their own because of the impressive and positive impact she makes wherever she lives and works. She is sought throughout the United States to speak, preach, and teach and has been the guest of governments in a number of countries in Africa, Europe, the Middle East, and the West Indies.

Barbara combines all of this background into her full-time position as a minister since founding Hillside. She serves as Chief Executive Officer and Chairperson of the Board of Trustees at Hillside, and is the Founder and President of the Barbara King School of Ministry.

Reverend King's dream for Hillside is manifesting annually. This independent church is an ecumenical ministry, a new-thinking church, founded on the teachings of Jesus Christ and the practical application of His Principles to everyday living. So popular and necessary are Barbara's messages, sermons, classes, and programs at Hillside, that the present facility is being expanded to include a $3 million "Church-in-the-Round" to accommodate the growth and ever-widening circle of members and friends who are uplifted by her ministry.

Barbara's messages in sermon, song, and books reflect the common theme that WITH GOD, ALL THINGS ARE POSSIBLE! Her life is a testimony; her church is a testimony; her work throughout the world is a testimony; this book is a testimony. Her family is a testimony—Barbara is the proud mother of a young adult son, Michael, with whom she shares a close relationship and who has been with her throughout the development of her ministry.

Barbara, often fondly called "Dr. Barbara," is someone special, someone who has a lingering presence, a comforting smile, a healing hand, a gentle touch. To so many, she is a minister, a teacher, a businesswoman, a counselor, a queen and king, a mother, a spiritual leader, a friend. That's why you hear it said, over and over again, that

"SHE IS IN STRIDE WITH THE UPPER PROGRESSIVE MOVEMENT OF LIFE, AND THE MARK OF SUCCESS IS UPON HER RIGHT NOW!

THANK YOU, FATHER!"